The Burden of Office
Agamemnon and Other Losers

THE BURDEN OF OFFICE

Agamemnon and Other Losers

Joseph Tussman

Talonbooks • Vancouver • 1989

published with the assistance of The British Columbia Civil
Liberties Association

Talonbooks
201/1019 East Cordova
Vancouver
British Columbia V6A 1M8
Canada

Typeset in Bem by Piéce de Résistance Ltée.; printed and bound
in Canada by Commercial Colour Press.

"Remembering Alexander Meiklejohn" appeared in *Liberal
Educator* (Winter 1984).

First printing: May 1989

Canadian Cataloguing in Publication Data

Tussman, Joseph, 1914—
   The burden of office, or, Agamemnon and
other losers

   ISBN 0-88922-265-7

   1. Authority. 2. Power (Social sciences).
3. Political science - Philosophy. 4. Politics
and literature. I. Title. II. Title:
Agamemnon and other losers.
HM271.T88 1989   303.3'6   C89-091307-2

CONTENTS

Foreword

Many years ago in a Berkeley restaurant, I heard Joe Tussman—then professor and head of the Philosophy Department at the University of California—describe himself as a man who had lived off the crumbs from Alexander Meiklejohn's table.

Meiklejohn was a distinctively American figure; an insider—President of Amherst, friend of both Woodrow Wilson and Justice Frankfurter—who spent the better part of his long life resisting developments, in the political and educational life of his country, that seemed both inevitable and sensible to his fellows. He publicly opposed, as did very few establishment figures, the McCarthyism of what his newspaperman friend, I.F. Stone, called the "Haunted Fifties." In 1955, he testified on the meaning of freedom of speech to a Senate Committee on the Judiciary, cooly informing that body that it was not enough that Americans were free to advocate a revolution in 1776—the First Amendment meant they were to be free *evermore* to *advocate* a revolution, be it Marxist or otherwise. And in 1957, he personally petitioned Congress to either disband the House Committee on UnAmerican Activities, or drastically truncate its mandate. Recognizing the "closing of the American mind" several generations before Alan Bloom wrote of it, he devoted his academic career to the liberal college, and reckoned the diminution of that centrally important educational institution as the great disappointment of his life. His philosophical treatment of the college and university in *Education Between Two Worlds* remains the single indispensable text on the mission of higher education in a democracy. Alexander Meiklejohn was a great man, and the fact that, by the time of his death in 1964, he had pretty thoroughly escaped being a famous man, tells us something about both the nature of fame and the absence of any personal ambition or egoism to leaven this austere Scot's passion for the truth.

Still, Tussman was wrong. That is, at least as far as his representation of himself as a pale copy of Meiklejohn goes, he was wrong. It may be true that, as Tussman mused during his own efforts to reform collegiate education at Berkeley during the sixties, he was "no Alexander Meiklejohn." But Tussman's works—*Obligation and the Body Politic* (1960), *Experiment at Berkeley* (1969), and *Government and the Mind* (1977)—certainly hold a place of honour of their own. And the book at hand, *The Burden of Office*, is, simply, a masterwork from a wise man at the height of his powers.

That such a conservative mind as that of Tussman could understand itself as deriving from, rather than reacting to, the liberal socialism of his great teacher, Meiklejohn, is a reflection on nutritive origins rather than pecking order. As Tussman is fond of insisting, the beginning of every story stands at the end of another. The reader may, however, form their own view of the relationship between the intellectual stories of these men from Tussman's memoir of Meiklejohn, which appears as an appendix to this volume.

The mention of stories is not unintentional. For *The Burden of Office* is a book in which Tussman takes up the great emblematic stories of the human task of governance— Agamemnon, Moses, Lear, Oedipus, Antigone—and offers fresh readings of them in an effort to understand the nature of political authority. He provides us with a text which is an

8

antidote for our chaotic times, which are more and more deeply marked by intellectual, moral, and political drift.

Indeed, one of the great gifts offered by Tussman in this book is the rescue of these ancient stories, so relegated to the sphere of "myth" (read fanciful stories, children's tales, matter not useful for rational adult thought) in this century that they are seldom taught to, much less understood by, the majority of us. Tussman's accomplishment in *The Burden of Office* is to restore these classics to their proper place in our working spiritual armoury, so that they can be deployed in our attempt to rescue ourselves from a vapid humanism on the one hand and facism on the other.

Tussman's thought is, as I have already suggested, conservative. The truth may seem to help us place him. We think we know how the dichotomy works: "A liberal is a conservative who has been arrested; and a conservative is a liberal who has been mugged by reality." But none of this off-the-rack conceptual workwear fits Tussman. Indeed, it simply leads us to a complete misunderstanding of him. His thought works at a depth that tends to make traditional identifying labels irrelevant.

It is true that he puts a Hobbesian premium on recognizing and conserving that which makes us governable. But that is simply because he wants democracy, or self-government, to both work and endure. It is possible to forget, he reminds us, that the vital idea of democracy—government *of* the people, *by* the people, *for* the people—does not constitute a form of escape from government. It simply reserves the ultimate governing authority for the citizenry. Meiklejohn, the great student of the American Constitution, gave pointed expression to this fact our political lives with his evocation of the people as the *fourth branch* of a democratic government. We are not ruled, he taught us, by the legislature, executive, and judicial branches: "these are but among the instruments we use in the governance of ourselves."

The citizen has ruling work to do that can never be delegated. We are, in a manner of speaking, never out of office. In fact, it is by virtue of its official status as the sovereign ruling

9

authority that a democratic citizenry lays claim to a range of civil rights—such as freedom of conscience, expression, and association—which secure for them the powers necessary for the performance of their political duties. We are not merely "consumers" of government; we have an official role to play in the provision of it. We all bear, however unselfconsciously, carelessly, or even unwittingly, the burden of office.

So, in case it should seem that Tussman's radical re-reading of their ancient stories brings an undemocratic sympathy to the cases of Lear and Moses and Agamemnon and Creon and the rest, remember that the object of the exercise is to consider the character of a burden that *we* have decided to take up. Creon's handling—or mismanagement—of Antigone's defiance of his burial edict is not merely an antic episode; it is a case study that ought to evoke our citizenly interest. A democratic government has to come to grips, as does *any* system of government, with the challenge to its rule posed by the civilly disobedient. Of course, we would never be so foolish as to issue such a headstrong or intemperate or downright stupid order as Creon's. Of course.

If two things are certain, it is that those who bear the burden of office are going to make mistakes . . . *and* that they are not going to be able to tell their mistakes from their strokes of ruling genius until it no longer matters which was which. One of the burdens of office is the certain knowledge that with the best of luck and the best of intentions, our best efforts are still going to yield some terrible blunders. And the companion burden to this one is the understanding that if our laws are to provide the authoritative direction to the life of the community that they must, there can be no "excepting" circumstances for the obedience demanded of the subjects. The burden of office is the burden of command.

Beyond the theme of the ruler as beautiful loser, this is a book which offers a criticism of some of the institutions that both support and compromise civilization. An affectionate criticism, I should immediately qualify, because Tussman sees the great institutions—such as marriage or the law—as giving an enduring form to essential human passions which would otherwise be as transient as their mortal source. "Marriage does for love what the law does for morality." Wreck it, you mutter? Tussman isn't unconditionally thrilled by the human condition, either. This is, after all, a criticism.

It is, however, a criticism offered by a man who once pointed out to me that no one could imagine a good film critic who hated films. Similarly, a critic of government or institutions who does not really love these things is an intellectual poseur who deserves a careful reading and a wide berth. So, when we hear, in Tussman's treatment of the *Oresteia*, that the courts do not offer us "a better solution" to the moral quandaries we bring to them, we are not to imagine that we are invited to a fresh kind of disrespect for the law. We are, rather, to meditate on the terrible furies that Athena saved us from with her invention of our legal antics. Due process, it turns out, does not simply protect the accused from an outraged public; it rescues us all from being inexorably drawn back to the place whence our rage comes from.

If the reader detects a whiff of Platonism here, it is no accident. Tussman agrees with the Greek that there is a profound relationship between the mastery of one's own life and the arts of governance. Plato, of course, believed that there would always be so many who could never achieve the rational governance of their own souls that we must look to the precious few "philosopher-kings" among us for the deliberative talent with which to rule the human city. He drew a deep dividing line between the very few fit to govern, and the very many fit only to be ruled. Tussman, the democrat, moves Plato's dividing line from *between* citizens—where it is obnoxious to us, and locates it *within* each citizen—where it hopefully ennobles. A democratic community is defined by its commitment to governance not by the best *among* all of us, but by the best *within* each of us. We have set ourselves free to bring a self-disciplined contribution to the collegial task of governing ourselves. It remains to be seen whether or not what Meiklejohn called "this experiment of democracy" will be successful.

Every democratic people has its carrot and its stick. The

carrot is the hope, the dream, the animating vision of a government of genuinely free women and men. The "Platonic form" of *self*-government. The stick, on the other hand, is the thousand different varieties of the Golden Calf, and Cordelia's expeditionary force, that wait like nightmares for democratic authority to nod. The staff of office is a tiger's tail.

A closing note of encouragement to the reader. Tussman wryly observed once that you must never ask an academic if he has read a particular classic. You have to ask him if he has *re-read* it recently. This is a book written by a man worldly enough to know that our time is not one that is steeped in the works of Aeschylus and the Old Testament. So relax. Tussman brings these stories in from the cold for everybody, and he has a beautiful knock.

John Dixon
President of the British Columbia Civil Liberties Association
Vancouver, British Columbia

Introduction

These are familiar stories. We all know that Agamemnon conquered Troy and then was killed by his wife in his homecoming bath, that King Lear had a terrible time with his daughters, that Oedipus killed his father and married his mother, that Antigone gave up her life in inventing civil disobedience, that Moses freed the Jews from slavery in Egypt and led them on their long march to the promised land. They are so familiar that it seems odd to be telling them again.

Nevertheless, I retell them, in fairly simple language, in our contemporary vernacular, as if they could, in essential respects, have happened today. I do not change the actual historical setting, but I treat the story as if, beneath the temporal guise or disguise, we find characters essentially like ourselves. This, of course, is to reject the "historical" approach—the view that we can understand an Orestes or a Creon only if we see him immersed in his own time and place responding to his own peculiarly local contexts in ways that are appropriate or even intelligible only in those contexts. But if we think we can understand what happened in Antigone only if we grasp a peculiarly Theban preoccupation with burial, then we have missed the point. I would argue, if I had to, that it is only when we see some things *out* of context that we really understand them. In any case, I tell the stories in their traditional settings. We find Lear in some sort of old England and I leave him there although, as a matter of fact, I ran into Goneril in Chicago.

I also tend to cut the characters down to size. I do not treat these as stories about creatures who are larger than life, about giants or monsters who once roamed the earth; they are about *us*. Who does not know an ambitious or dedicated man—or woman—who has sacrificed a child on the altar of a career? Our world teems with Agamemnons and Iphigenias, with Clytemnestras and Orestes.

Nor, if they are not larger than life, are they clearer or simpler or easier to "read" when we meet them in the text than when we encounter them in the flesh. We are entitled to be as baffled by the action of Cordelia in Act I, Scene I, as by the behavior of our neighbor's daughter who makes a scene at some ceremony; and differing interpretations can be defended to the edge of complete misunderstanding. If these characters are indeed like us, they are, as we are, a bit mysterious, never fully understood.

But why, you may ask, bother with these stories at all? If I were not in the process of shedding my ill-fitting academic garb I would reply by trying to explain about the humanities. About how the humanities are those studies that, unlike the sciences, take the distinctively human categories—purpose and obligation for example—seriously; that the "story" is the basic humanistic unit; that understanding ourselves is grasping the plots in which we play a part; that these stories are fairly elemental and have a special role in our education. But while this is all true and deserves to be argued—elsewhere—the justification for this telling of these stories is that you, the reader, may be as entertained, stimulated, and even edified in reading them as I have been in writing them. I aim primarily at your pleasure, only insidiously at other things.

Two themes emerge irrepressibly from these retold tales. The first is about tragedy and "the burden of office." The second is about the civilizing or taming of the passions.

THE BURDEN OF OFFICE

This is not an age disposed to celebrate the mystery of the very idea of "office." "Official" is, with us, almost a derogatory or comic term. What intrigues us is the person, the private person, the "real" person lurking half-concealed behind a facade. Have we forgotten that "person" comes (the dictionary will tell us) from "persona" meaning "mask," therefore the character played by an actor, not the actor himself—poor clod, far less than the king he impersonates? Well, whatever things used to mean, we know what we think now. On one hand there is the role, the functionary, the officer, the official—someone putting on an act; on the other hand, if he would only be himself, is the private human being—just folks, real people. We like to transcend roles and meet person to person, to step outside the office for a face-to-face encounter; we have an ingrained aversion to officialdom, to officialese, a romantic urge to puncture the pomp of ceremony and face the world and each other with shining private faces.

So I cannot assume that we do indeed appreciate the mystery of office or appreciate the achievement of subduing power into the holding of an office, of taming (or trying to tame) the ruler into an official—into a person with duties and obligations, not merely an insatiable center of gigantic appetites, a person with things to do that may be the death of his private self, that may make the office seem less an opportunity than a burden. And sometimes, even without the aid of flaws, a tragic burden. In fact, if we do not understand the office and its burdens we may not understand about tragedy.

Let me distinguish two kinds of tension or conflict built in to the office of the ruler, both very familiar. First, between the private interests of the ruler and his public duty, his obligation to serve the public interest of the group of which he is ruler. We are all too familiar with this in a banal form as a "conflict of interest" and we have our share of depressing scandals involving officials who, in one way or another, manage to line their private nests with public feathers. These are merely sordid episodes and rise to a poignant level only when an otherwise great career is brought to ruin by a kind of kleptomaniac flaw. Ah, but for that, we murmur, shaking our heads . . . . But we are more likely to consider it a pity rather than a tragedy, a weakness in the face of temptation, a case of wrong-doing even if a bit inexplicable or disproportionate. Not quite tragic.

But there are other conflicts in which it is not the prospect of private gain that tempts one from his duty, but the threat of private or personal disaster. It is still a conflict between public duty and private interest or value, but duty sometimes exacts a price beyond the mere forgoing of gain. It was in his role as leader of the Greek expedition that Agamemnon was required to sacrifice his daughter; it was as ruler of Thebes that Oedipus was bound to expose the killer of King Laius; it was as the ruler of a strife-torn city that Creon broke his son's heart by enforcing his loyalty law against Antigone. I suppose someone could be found who would argue that civic diligence, the sense of duty, is the root of the trouble—the tragic flaw. Without it, Agamemnon would have hugged Iphiginea, called off the expedition, and allowed Helen to die of boredom in Troy. Oedipus might have heeded Jocasta's advice, dropped the investigation, and lived happily ever after with his motherly wife and their children. Creon (although if Oedipus had been sensible we would not have heard of him) might have heeded his son's pleas, pardoned Antigone, accepted her as daughter-in-law in spite of his foreboding, and lived to enjoy his grandchildren. If only they had not taken the duties of office so seriously!

But there is another deep source of conflict built into the office of the ruler, besides the conflict between the ruler's duty and his private interests. It is the conflict between what the public good requires and what the public happens to want. Or perhaps I should say, between what the ruler thinks the public good requires and what the public wants, or thinks it wants, or even thinks is good for it. The office of the ruler sometimes seems to involve, however we may state it, getting the ruled to do what they don't want to do.

Parents and teachers are familiar with the difficulties of

getting people to do what they may not want to do even if it is good for them. We coax, scare, inspire, outfox, manipulate, bribe, flatter, cajole—all this to get someone to do something he does not want to do. We do this for a variety of motives. Sometimes, for our own purposes; sometimes for a purpose in the benefits of which they may have a share; sometimes the motive may be, predominantly, the benefit of the manipulated. To justify getting people to do what they do not feel like doing is a messy business, full of uncertainty, open to charges of deception and self-deception, to cynicism and hypocrisy. But it is difficult, nevertheless, to describe leadership or the office of the leader without recognizing that sometimes the leader is called upon to waken his followers, to stir them from lethargy and lead or drive them along a path they might not choose if left to themselves, to lead them into dubious battles on dubious journeys towards dubious promised lands.

It is inevitable, therefore, that there will be conflicts between leaders and followers. The leader will learn that he cannot rely on love alone. He will become less lovable, more fearsome, more distant, more forbidding. More like Moses. When the goal is clearly shared, much may be forgiven. But all too often the goal, the end, the vision, is not fully shared, not fully grasped not equally understood. We may march together under the banner of freedom, but to some "freedom" may mean only the release from immediate fetters, to others it may mean the achievement of the arts of self-mastery, of self-government. Sooner or later such a misunderstanding will lead to a quarrel over diverging paths, and we will experience again some version of the confrontation between the austere vision of the tablets of the law and the delicious temptations of the golden calf.

Moses, of course, is the great example of the leader whose vision is not fully shared. But he does not stand alone, even in our small sample. Lear had a vision of life based on equality, peace, and love—a vision, it turned out, not fully shared. And soon, love having failed, he was threatening—a bit too late—to call on terror. Agamemnon was told by Thersites on the plains of Troy that the troops did not share his Zeus-inspired vision of the war. Nor, he was to discover, did his wife. Creon's vision of a city firm and unified by loyalty left his divided city unmoved. Oedipus stood almost alone in his zeal for justice.

It is an old and universal story. Not only does the leader have to struggle against his own interest and inclinations in the performance of his office. He must also try to get people to do what they should do (alas, what he *thinks* they should do!) even if they don't want to. He may make mistakes. He may have flaws. But neither mistakes nor flaws are needed to account for his tragic fate. Tragedy is simply an aspect of the burden of office.

CIVILIZATION AND THE PASSIONS

The double nature of the powers with which we are involved sets the terms of the problem. The sun that brings us life can be the death of us. The oxygen we need can reduce us to ashes. The rain nourishes and drowns us in its floods. The facts of life! What we cannot live without can destroy us. We must learn to propitiate the powers we evoke.

What is so obvious about the great natural or impersonal forces is also true about the great human passions. On the one hand, necessary; on the other hand, destructive. Let me mention some of the central powers or passions that bless and bedevil us.

Eros

Obviously one of the forces to which we owe our lives, without which, operating at a pre-reflective level, we would not be here. Powerful, necessary, the root of self-transcendence, of the varieties of love and all that we value flowing from that. And yet, a source of anguish, of misery, of torment, of unhappiness, of conflict, madness, murder, war. Half of wisdom is learning to tiptoe in the presence of eros.

Indignation, Fury, Moral Fervor

Difficult to name, but clearly the Greeks were on to

something about the Furies. Moral passion, stirred by an offense to the sense of justice. A deeply instinctive reaction to something that threatens *us*, the social group, the basic human unit. Its absence—indifference, genuine carelessness—is a fatal disease. Its moderate presence supports the justice that makes trust and cooperation possible. Its raging presence brings fanatical or holy war, the horrors of unslaked vengeance, the interminable feud.

Curiosity

Too mild a name for the cognitive lust, the thirst to know. Without it, no knowledge, no science, no arts, no power. But feared today as the human passion that may bring us to the end of the world. In its grip we stop at nothing, recognizing no forbidden fruit, undeterred by decency. In its grip, in popular imagination, one sells one's soul to the devil.

Acquisitiveness

If we do not leap to a pejorative sense we see that it begins as a kind of prudent concern to get what we need to satisfy our wants, now and in the future, to provide for ourselves, our families, our friends, our fellows. To save ourselves by being more like ants than like grasshoppers, to evoke and direct energy, to store up for tomorrow or for a rainy day. It is simple prudence, an adjunct to productivity, a necessary virtue. But, carried away, we can become misers, acquire the Midas touch, turn ugly with greed, cupidity, avarice—transforming a virtue into a destructive vice.

Pride

At one end of the scale we find something desirable and necessary—proper pride, self respect, a sense of dignity, the capacity to know shame, to feel disgrace. At the other end we encounter the thirst for fame, for status, for glory—the arrogance, the heedless autonomy, the pride that goes before a fall. The one, a precondition of civility; the other, a prelude to disaster.

I do not attempt to list these in order of significance, to dissect their complexities, to present anything like a complete list of deadly benign forces. They are a central handful of the great powers or passions crucial to our well-being and our misery; gods to be evoked with care lest they destroy us.

There is a great tradition that offers us, at this point, salvation through moderation. Not too little; not too much; just the right amount. Avoid extremes, seek balance. We are to be neither monkish nor libertine, neither indifferent nor fanatical, neither ignorant nor over-inquisitive, neither improvident nor greedy, neither without self-respect nor driven by vanity or pride. Neither a teetotaler nor a drunkard be—about any of the great passions. I do not intend to quarrel with this advice, but I have a different point to make.

The clue is presented most clearly in Orestes. Fury, moral outrage, the demand for justice cannot simply be moderated, toned down, made less urgent—as if we are to achieve the right degree of indignation, indignation dampened by a dose of indifference, carefully mixed to produce just the right strength of moral outrage. We enter, instead, an arena in which a special game with its own set of rules is to be played. Moral indignation gives way to legal argument; fury is tied in legal knots—trapped, confined, restrained, transformed, tamed. The passion finds itself institutionalized, learns to express itself in a set of appropriate habits. Impulse and intuition give way to bureaucracy. Morality bows to legality. War gives way to the rule of law. We become civilized.

The story of fury and its taming into law is the story of all the great passions. We develop the forms within which they are both recognized, acknowledged, satisfied and, nevertheless, banked, kept within limits, restrained. We learn how to live with them—using them, (and we *do* need them) while we keep them from destroying us. Not perfectly, of course. There are disasters lurking everywhere, and sometimes we meet them. But we tame our passions within habits and institutions—habits writ large. And they take many forms.

If civilization generally requires or even survives by "institutionalization," any particular civilization or culture is a particular way of taking shape. Thus, eros makes its universal and undeniable claims and is trained into a variety of forms. Marriage, for example. Monogamous, polygamous, dissoluble, indissoluble, strict or tolerant of a variety of quasi-legitimate supportive infidelities. In its most assertive mood, the institution of marriage aspires to a total monopoly of legitimate sexuality. A rather daring claim, not unlike the claim of the institutions of the sovereign to a monopoly of legitimate coercive power, and honored only to a degree. But the point is that marriage and its ancillary institutions are cultural attempts to tame eros into a benign form. The pattern may vary from culture to culture and from time to time, but every human group will erect its temples and shrines for this deity.

As with eros, so it is with all the great passions. The Oresteia is, as I have mentioned, deliberately explicit in its celebration of the civilizing of moral passion within the framework of law, of the subordination of fury to due process. The habit of going to court, of submitting to its judgement, is to supplant the life (and death!) of raging righteousness.

The passion for knowledge may not seem to belong in this fevered company, and may not seem to need restraining. At least it may not seem so in the academic world where we commonly worry more about kindling the passion than dampening it. But there is a long tradition of fear of the mad scientist with his unquenchable thirst—Faust and all those restless probing minds uncovering the secrets of the atom, of the genetic code, of the mind, of the soul, of all that heady fruit the taste of which may threaten what remains of innocence. In spite of bold claims to freedom, however, even the pursuit of truth is subject to social and political constraint. Much of it could not even go on without governmental sanction and support. A university may require that anyone doing research on human subjects must get the approval of a committee. Even animals are now protected by committees against abuse by decent human beings in the grip of the urge to know. The

21

cognitive passion is not an exception to the rule that the great passions need institutional constraint. Essentially it lives within and is governed by the academy.

Acquisitiveness? We give it the marketplace and the casino as playgrounds. It is legitimate there, but even there it feels the rein and the curb, the constraints of its institutions.

Pride? Beset by ceremony, by ribbons and laurel wreaths, by the severity of honor . . . .

But I am getting tired of laboring the obvious. Let me sum up. Civilization requires the institutionalization of the necessary but dangerous passions. Any civilization is a particular way of doing so, achieving—growing into—its complex forms by more or less happy accident. To describe a culture is to map the structure of its institutions. To criticize or evaluate a culture is to judge the adequacy of its institutions in the light of some conception of how the various passions can best be expressed or shaped or harnessed to serve a variety of human purposes.

The fundamental relation between passions and institutions gives rise to two pervasive attitudes—three, if we consider sanity an attitude: Romanticism, Puritanism, and, for want of a better name, Classicism.

Romanticism is the desire or tendency to liberate the passions from the constraints of their controlling institutions—the belief that salvation lies in this form of liberation. It is usually selective. Thus, there are justice-romantics who think that the legal system cramps, spoils, distorts justice, who think that it would be better to burst out of or put aside the absurd, the artificial constraints of mere legality and live directly by our innate sense of justice, our natural indignation, our uncomplicated moral sense. Just do what you think is right; let your conscience be your guide. Free morality from the distorted or warped demands of legality and we will be saved!

Predictably, there are eros-romantics who believe that if we would only free love from the cramping institutions within which we imprison it, all will be well. Saved by love unleashed! There are greed-romantics (to be unfair about it) who believe that if we free self-interest from its bonds, free acquisitiveness or even avarice (that's what *you* call it!) from foolish idealistic restraint, we would end up running happily, barefooted, through lush layers of gross national product. There are cognitive-romantics who believe that if only we would free the quest for truth from its bondage to the academy, the tenured professoriate, The National Academy of Establishment Clods, we, the unlicensed maverick learners would discover, driven by pure curiosity, all the wonderful things the world contains, especially the deeper truths about society. And so on . . . .

Romanticism is an attitude found most charmingly in the young, aware of the passions in their freshness, not yet much acquainted with the dark side of the world. Charming, as one of Plato's characters says, as a lisp might be in the young, unseemly in the old. Not surprising in Cordelia, unforgivable in Lear. Romanticism is a persisting, ever-recurring view of things. If it is not saved from itself, it is doomed to a belated disillusionment. The message is short: free us from the artificial restraint of habit and institution and we will enter the promised land.

Puritanism by contrast is marked by a deep distrust of the passions. The puritan instinct is, as far as possible, to get rid of, to extirpate the troublesome passions, to de-legitimize their claims, not to respect them or give them scope. If that cannot, alas, be done, the puritan will seek to confine them within a grudging framework. I need not remind anyone of the familiar story of puritanism and eros, but some of the other manifestations of the puritan spirit may be less familiar, less easily recognized. There are puritans about the shameless thirst for justice who now say about punishment all the things they used to say about sex. Not for them the enjoyment, the delight of the sight of justice done, of fitting retribution, of indignation satisfied. No! That is a crude lust, an ignoble feeling, an expression of our lower nature, something to be suppressed, conquered, to be ashamed of. So much for the deep human desire to have the world give people what they deserve! Wisdom aside, this is a form of puritanism in which the sexually liberated slake their displaced puritan urge. There are some oddities about this. One person may be a romantic about sex and a puritan about justice; another may be a puritan about sex and a romantic about punishment or justice. We are seldom romantics or puritans across the board; we are selective in revealing ways. (Try this out: what kind of people tolerate pornography and oppose capital punishment? What kind hate pornography and approve of capital punishment? Which calls what "obscene"?)

I risk mentioning that socialism seems to be, in some respects, the opposite number to greed-romanticism. That is, it is an expression of the puritan spirit with respect to acquisitiveness, to the "profit motive"—motives or passions held in low repute, seen as an expression of our lower nature, as compared with, more nobly, acting directly in the service of "needs" or higher aspirations.

Finally, I mention cognitive puritanism. I am not thinking of the purist who disdains idle speculation, who believes in not venturing beyond the bare facts, who won't accept what has not been confirmed by a properly controlled study, who, in short, disciplines his curiosity. I refer rather to those who have never forgiven Eve or Pandora, who think that the passion to know has produced more ill than good, who think that simple virtue is wisdom enough, that the world was meant to be full of secrets, that the desire to know threatens the environment, that there is no "right" to know that goes beyond the absolute need to know, that we are better off when universities are few, small, and poor, that research budgets, except when clearly under the control of people who don't care about knowledge for its own sake, should be cut to the bone. Cognitive puritans.

What I will call the classical view, as a bow to the Greeks who seem so imbued with it, respects the passions and is reluctant to deny any its due. (Alas for poor Pentheus who had no respect for Bacchus.) The classical mind recognizes the double-edged quality of the great forces and recognizes that they must be embodied in suitable institutions whose ceremonies must be honored. It seeks neither to extirpate the passion nor to abolish the institution. It recognizes that civilization is an achievement in the face of difficulties, a precarious achievement. It is the state of mind of the magician who tremblingly invokes the powers he would use, knowing that if he gets the ceremony wrong what he invokes will destroy him. Neither romantic nor puritan; merely sensible.

These two themes—the burden of office and the taming of the passions—pervade the tales retold here. But nothing really turns on this being the case, and the tales were not selected to illustrate anything. I will resist the temptation to elaborate on the relation between the themes and the tales, to make sure that you don't miss all the subtleties and profound insights. It is best, I think, to simply take these as they come, without trying to think *about* them, or worrying about missing the point.

The Orestes Case

Orestes was a young man who killed his mother. Not by accident nor in a fit of rage but deliberately. There was never any doubt about whether he did it, but there was some doubt about what should be done with him. The case involved a very prominent family and became the center of heated political controversy. In fact, it is hard to tell where the domestic drama ends and the political drama begins.

The mother, when she was murdered (punished, some said), was already quite famous. She was the sister of Helen (Helen of Troy, we are tempted to say, but she was *not* a Trojan) and had been married to Agamemnon who, as everyone knows, was the leader of the Greek expedition against Troy. Agamemnon returned victorious and was promptly murdered by his wife, Clytemnestra, the mother of our Orestes. She gave all sorts of reasons. Whatever the reasons, or pretexts, or justifications, she killed him and, with her lover, whom she married, ruled over the city. She was a strong woman.

Orestes was not around when his father was killed. He had been sent away and grew up in exile, if a child can be said to be in exile. We really know very little about this period of his life. It is clear, however, that he did not forget his father, or his mother. He came to see himself as his father's avenger. Eventually, he returned to his childhood home, covertly, with a plan. He carried it out. That is, he killed his step-father and, in cold blood, with his own hands, he killed his mother.

Whatever plans he may have had of settling into his father's place immediately went awry. He fled and became a refugee with a reputation, a moving center of controversy. Everywhere he went he found supporters and critics, but no peace, no absolution. He was a cause célèbre. Finally, at Athens, a court was established to try his case, and cases like it. He was tried and acquitted.

The best account of the Orestes case—I suppose we must call it that although he is the least interesting character in it—is given by Aeschylus in the *Oresteia*. He presents it in three parts. In *Agamemnon*, the returned conqueror is killed by Clytemnestra. Next, in the *Libation Bearers* we are introduced to Orestes and taken through the killing of his mother. Finally, the trial and all that occurs in the *Eumenides*.

Aeschylus presented the *Oresteia* in 458 BC. It was one of those early entries in the annals of crime we think of as tragedies—crises that have entered deeply into our consciousness, that ring bitter changes on the way in which what is designed to support us can destroy us. Orestes, who merely killed his mother, is not as famous as his countryman, Oedipus, who killed his father and married his mother. Nor even as famous as Antigone, the iron-willed young woman whose original venture in civil disobedience is still celebrated. But Orestes is still remembered. He is, after all, the only son of Agamemnon, who is quite unforgettable. Agamemnon is seldom given his full due. He is easily misunderstood, easily disliked, easily ridiculed. It is nice that his son, at least, idolized him. Orestes serves as the model of the son who punishes his mother because she, as a bad wife, is the undoing of her husband, the boy's hero-father. He gets even for daddy. A useful type.

But the story, bloody as it is, also carries a message. The *Eumenides* is not only the account of the trial, it is also a commentary—Aeschylus's commentary—on the world, on the quality of justice, on the havoc of moral indignation. Justice, we will see, is put in its place.

I. AGAMEMNON

The watchman on the roof is waiting for the signal. He is weary, trying to keep awake, grudgingly impressed with the ingenuity of the system, brooding about how things have been going downhill. He was left behind with the too-old and the too-young when the fleet sailed ten years ago. Sated with rumors, resigned to home-front scandal, he longs for the end of the war. And now, finally, at last! The signal! They are coming home. Good news, for some; bad news, for others. Let us rejoice! But carefully, carefully.

The opening notes are bittersweet, a mixture of joy and apprehension. The signal itself, a relay of fire leaping from peak to peak, is oddly ambiguous. Are we reminded of victory fireworks? Of warning flares? Does it say rejoice, we have won? Does it say get ready, they are coming? Someone has set up an elaborate early warning system. The thought of Agamemnon worries two cities.

The sense of doubleness deepens. Clytemnestra, the queen left in charge, summons up a vision of conquered Troy: the Greeks, now unopposed, ranging triumphantly at will, loose, ravenous; the Trojans bent, weeping over their dead among the ashes of their lives. Conqueror and conquered in one city, she imagines, like oil and vinegar in a single jar. Sweet victory. Bitter defeat.

So it is V-Day. This time, in Argos. It is the first day of the post-war world, the eve of homecoming. Some will return as ashes in small urns; some in the flesh, hardened, changed. But home has changed too. Nothing will ever be the same. Nor, in a world of veterans, can everything be fresh and new. The new day dawns on an old world. It is the day of victory; it is the day of reckoning. We are now waiting for Agamemnon.

While we wait, the background is sketched in. Paris had run off to Troy, his home, with Helen. Menelaus, the forsaken husband, appeals to his brother, Agamemnon, who gathers a Greek expedition against Troy. But before it can sail,

28

Agamemnon is required to sacrifice his daughter, Iphigenia. He makes the sacrifice, they sail, a ten-year campaign ensues—at the end of which Troy is destroyed—and now it is over. Simple enough to tell; not so easy to understand. What kind of monster is Agamemnon? What is the war really all about? And what, if there is a point, is the point of the sacrifice?

First, the war. We look for the cause. Not the cause *of* it; the cause *in* it. We fight, we say, because they crossed the Nth parallel. But the "cause" in which we are fighting may be the integrity of frontiers, or the curbing of aggression, or the sanctity of treaties. The concrete occasion does not exhaust the deeper issue; it may barely exemplify it; and it may evoke a response that seems, if we are blind to the issue, grossly disproportionate.

"Zeus, god of hospitality, sent the sons of Atreus against Paris, because a woman was not content with one husband." Zeus is the issue; Helen is only the event. But let us first give Helen her due. Beautiful Helen. Really beautiful, too beautiful to stay hidden in a provincial town, reserved for the adoration of her bucolic husband. She falls in love with Paris—handsome, foreign, sophisticated, much-courted, irresistible Paris. She hangs on his tales of Troy. The broad avenues, the high-rising towers, the glittering international set, the brilliant parties. It is hard to imagine Paris intense about anything. He is good natured, he laughs, and he carries back to Troy a plague disguised as a lovely woman. Of course they will not extradite her; they would rather die first. Naturally, she becomes bored, gets a bit homesick, and, as is her habit, betrays her shelter to besiegers and, unscathed, still beautiful, goes back to Menelaus.

What a price to pay! What a long, stupid, bloody, pointless war! "A boy runs after a fluttering bird and puts affliction into ten thousand lives." Helen is restless and so "the broken wall, the burning roof and tower, and Agamemnon dead . . . ." What has Zeus—whatever that may be, mutters Aeschylus—what has Zeus got to do with all this?

War reveals itself differently to each of our three selves—to our plebeian, our heroic, and our Olympian natures. Our plebeian view, our view from below, the view of the rank and file, the lower echelon, the eternal GI is always the same.

Cramped journeys, the winter's cold, the summer's heat, the food, the bugs, the monotony, the turmoil and confusion, the risk of life and limb, the sudden disaster, the near miss, the lucky interlude, the comic inefficiency, the senselessness of the little picture—endured with stoicism, with humor, with camaraderie, loyalty, courage, and endless grumbling patience. Reality is cold, wet, dangerous. Issues are remote abstractions, the "cause" a bitter jest. Peace is going home.

To our heroic selves war is the great test. It is the test of courage, skill, power, honor; a quest for victory and glory. The Greeks beat the Trojans. Achilles beats Hector. Wellington won. Montgomery chased the Desert Fox. MacArthur returned. The story line soars above the mud; it hardly notices the issues—well, perhaps issues provide banners. It is personal. How I prepared, how I persevered through the dry years, how the moment came, how I was ready, how I won, how I behaved with magnanimity . . . . To the heroic view, war, life, is an adventure story. Peace is an interlude for training, a time between engagements.

So we come to Zeus and the Olympian view, to the level at which invisible things wait to be grasped by the mind, where eyes do not help, where "I see" means "I understand," where we find significance. Paris stole Helen; or rather, hospitality was abused. Infatuated Helen deserted Menelaus; that is, love betrayed and desolated the hearth. Zeus—god, principle, power of hospitality—summoned Agamemnon . . . . Hera, Zeus' wife, protector of home and hearth, was determined to assert supremacy over Aphrodite, to subordinate the erotic to the domestic. Homer disguises the higher politics as Olympian comedy. But the point is clear. We are in the presence of the great cultural struggle over the subordination of the libido to the structure of the family, the domestication of sex, the civilizing of one of the greatest of forces which, if disciplined, gives us Zeus and Hera, home and family, and all that means to mankind, and which, uncurbed, gives us instead merely Aphrodite and her favorite playmate, Ares—those ancient bedfellows, love and war. The Trojan war, seen from Olympus, is a deep crisis of civilazation.

Which of our selves is our deepest self? Which of the different worlds we glimpse, inhabit, is the deepest world? Have we not heard at least three answers? But this is the Age of the Lower Echelon (is it not?) and we glorify the view from the ranks. What is most real is what is most real to the eternal private in each of us. The misery, the wounds, death, are overwhelmingly, exclusively real. Honor? Glory? Are they not, we say, the destructive obsession of a line of adolescents from Achilles through Patton? And politics? The higher politics? You mean making the world safe for democracy? The Atlantic Charter? Anti-fascism? Human rights? Freedom? The holy principles of our new revolution? Words, just words, we say, hating Olympus, glowing with street-wise enlightenment as we vote to bring the legions home and beat their weapons into consumer goods.

It is hard, in such an age, to speak of higher issues without derision. Nevertheless! We really don't know what is going on, on the plain before Troy, or on any plain, unless we know what is happening on Olympus. We cannot understand a fuss about hostages, fewer than a day's traffic toll, unless we understand about the sanctity of heralds and embassies and international law (Hermes and Zeus) and all those other higher political sanctities, which from time to time, marshal rank and file behind aspiring heroes moving, at the command of statesmen, to vindicate the moral order. There *is* Olympus. But the dust from the plain sometimes obscures the view.

We cannot understand Agamemnon unless we can understand war, the war, his war. He is the leader of the expedition that made the Greeks, as Moses is the leader of the long march that made the Jews. Agamemnon is not like the watchman or the herald or the soldier. He is not like Hector or Achilles. He is the anointed leader in the service of Olympus, summoned to a just war.

The expedition is ready, but before Agamemnon can be Moses he is required to be Abraham. He is called upon to sacrifice his beloved child, the innocent Iphigenia. What is that all about?

The moral authority, the priest, Calchas, interprets the omens. Eagles are seen feasting on a hare and its unborn litter. So, the eagle sons of Atreus will destroy Troy. But they will destroy not only Paris and his defenders but the innocent as well—innocent victims, innocent bystanders, innocent children. Therefore, Artemis is angry. Artemis, protector of the cubs, the children, the innocent. She makes her demand. There must be a tribute to innocence. You cannot destroy the innocent, *their* innocent, without first offering up your own.

It is an amazing demand. You cannot just rush off to war heedless of everything but the cause, full of fury, swelling with righteous indignation. Stop! Consider the innocent! All right . . . I've considered them. I'm very sorry. No, that's not good enough. Think of your daughter. You can't bear the thought of her dead—so young, so tender, so innocent? Then you can't launch the war. The leader who sounds the trumpet of destruction must himself fully realize what it means. Therefore Iphigenia. No sacrifice, no war. But what of Zeus? Yes, there is Zeus. And he is higher than Artemis. But before you go on Zeus' errand you must bow to Artemis. You, the leader, must bow. You cannot delegate this ceremony.

Here is the central crisis of Agamemnon's life, the turning point in more stories than his own. No sacrifice, no war. But the war is necessary, the war is just. So . . .? It is recorded that he struggled, that bitterly he hurled the royal staff to the ground, that he refused. He did not move like Abraham, a knight of faith, without hesitation. He struggled. But in the end he did not refuse. He trampled on his fatherhood, turned his own home into a deathtrap, and, summoned by Zeus, went off to vindicate the sanctity of the home.

How can we, how dare we judge him unless we can understand war and sacrifice, unless we can imagine, or remember, a war whose leader we would condemn if he called it off for Artemis. Are we to be forever hostage to the innocents in their playpens among the spreading tents of wickedness? Are we always to turn our backs to the beaches of Normandy? Must virtue always defer to innocence?

The sacrifice crisis is about two different things. About Artemis, and about kingship; about innocents and about leadership. Agamemnon is forced to choose between the failure of the expedition and the life of his child; between what his public office requires and his fatherly love; between king and paterfamilias; between public duty and private desire. A conflict of interest. A tragic situation.

There is, in the early part of Plato's *Republic*, a famous argument between Socrates and a hard-boiled realist named Thrasymachus. Socrates argues that the function of the ruler is to take care of the interests of the public, the subjects, the weak, not to provide for the interests of the ruler, the interests of the stronger. How naive, retorts Thrasymachus. Everyone is always in business for himself, looking after number one . . . . The wonder is, how can anyone, if he is a creature bound, as seems natural and inevitable, to look after himself, ignore his own interests, subdue his private self to the duties of roles, functions, offices which serve interests other than his own, even opposed to his own. Who would be king if the king must pay?

Agamemnon. He is caught in the conflict and, in the end, is destroyed by it. But he does what he is supposed to do. He sacrifices his child (how many ways there are to sacrifice children!) and becomes the father of his country. He accepts the deep anguish of the personal loss. An unbelievable act, paying that price when it is presented concretely, not as an abstract possibility of a future loss, not as a projected casualty estimate. He does it. Horrible. Inhuman. Kingly. Agamemnon is terrifying. No wonder Clytemnestra sets up an early warning system against his return.

But now he does not have much longer to live. The war is over. He has made it home. He is allowed a glimpse, but he will not be allowed to dwell in that promised land. Greetings. A brief exchange. He goes to his bath (what can he wash away?) and is slaughtered, sacrificed to domestic fury.

Agamemnon's opening speech reveals how completely he has been taken over by his public role. There is nothing personal in it. First, he thanks the gods for helping him destroy Troy and making right prevail. Then he thanks the people for their promise of loyal support and adds some disillusioned remarks about the rarity of real loyalty. Only Odysseus, in fact . . . . Then he promises to deal promptly with the problems that must be piled up waiting for him. Believe me, there will be action! Then he announces that he is going into his palace to thank the gods who have brought him safely back. He does not mention Mrs. Agamemnon.

Clytemnestra's greeting, in stark contrast, is purely personal. She apologizes to the crowd for the coming display of emotion and launches into a sustained wail. It's been awful! Alone, without my husband all these years. The rumors! You're dead, you're wounded . . . the nightmares, the worry. I cried myself to sleep so often I'm out of tears. I had to send our son away in case you were killed and he'd be in danger. It's been just terrible! And now, thank god, you're back. Come into the house. But wait! My hero shouldn't step on the dirt. Step on these gorgeous tapestries I've made for you. You deserve it!

Much has been made of the purple-carpet reception and of the significance of Agamemnon's treading the deluxe path. It is another bad thing that Agamemnon does. He kills his daughter, he destroys Troy, and now, failing the test of pride, allows himself to trample on finery, too good to walk, like a mere mortal, on the bare earth. See, the man who crushed Troy has no respect for delicate things and next he may crush you!

It is a public relations skirmish. Agamemnon reacts like a politician with an eye to public opinion. Stop all this fussing, this extravagant display, he says. People will resent it, and their opinion is important. Don't treat me like a god or an Oriental despot. I'm a simple Greek king with simple tastes. Oh well, if it means so much to you. But at least let me take my shoes off. He gives in. He has not resisted very hard. He goes through with the lavish reception after all. The city has suffered years of deprivation; it is still in the midst of anxiety and mourning. But for the callous conqueror a costly, ostentatious reception. It was clever of Clytemnestra.

She has contrived for Agamemnon a foolish exit. We, standing in the crowd, see him stoop to fumble with his sandals. He straightens up, waves uncertainly, turns his back and moves, limping slightly, towards the stairway. And up, his bare feet uncertain among strange carpets, careful, clumsy, hesitant. His back, bent a bit since we saw it when he sailed away, disappears through the doorway. Clytemnestra follows.

But who is she, this weaver of plots, this assassin? She is another of Leda's daughters, Helen's sister (half-sister, if we credit the story of the swan evoked by Helen's slim-necked beauty). She is the plain sister, growing up in Helen's shadow; more intelligent, less flighty, less vain. The two sisters marry two royal brothers. Clytemnestra gets Agamemnon, a better catch, older, more powerful. Helen settles for Menelaus. Clytemnestra has three children, two girls and a boy. Helen has a daughter and, bored in Sparta, runs away with Paris. So far, the story of the good plain sister and the bad (bad? naughty?) beautiful sister. But from now on, life has it in for the good plain sister.

Her husband is called to pursue Helen. She cannot dissuade him. It's not just Helen, he says. There is a mutual assistance pact, the Greek alliance, a budding sense of unity against the East and its flagrant contempt for our way of life, the last straw, the end of appeasement, a matter of principle . . . . She does not have much use for all this "new politics." But her husband is seduced by it; her daughter is offered up to it; and she is left desolate in the shattered home, expected to behave like a general's wife and a gold-star mother.

Clytemnestra is domestic, not political. She is a wife and a mother, unmoved by "the cause." She even weeps for the Trojans; she sees them as husbands, brothers, fathers, children. For her, the human unit is the family. She is a casualty in its war against the presumptuous and intrusive state. Her husband may marshal civic power in aid of Zeus and Hera and the principles of marriage and home in general. She cares about her family in particular. So, when Agamemnon returns as first citizen she will not stand with dignity to greet him as first lady. She deliberately (was it not deliberate, studied?) confronts him with an hysterical wife. She does not kill him for political reasons, but against politics. When she displays Agamemnon dead (so much blood for a hollow man!) the fury, long smoldering, flares up. Iphigenia! Clytemnestra is the avenging mother.

But why does she also kill Cassandra? "Take care of her," Agamemnon had said as he turned to enter the house, "the troops gave her to me as a prize." He would have said the same thing if she had been a horse. An official decoration. Nothing really personal. Poor Cassandra. A Trojan girl, sensitive, fearful, prophetic, always scenting trouble, never taken seriously, living in a dream in which she always knows that something terrible is going to happen, and it does, and no one listens. The captive daughter of the losing king, a war victim. She might, in better times, have been a friend for Iphigenia. Now, she is butchered casually by Clytemnestra. Why? Jealousy is hardly an admissible plea. It is an act of vandalism against Agamemnon's trophy.

And now we learn, of course, that Clytemnestra has a lover. We accept the appearance of Aegisthus in that role with a mildly cynical shrug. So the good plain sister has a bit of Helen in her. Another betrayal. As lover, Aegisthus rounds out the domestic story of Agamemnon and Clytemnestra—he is the suitor accepted. The mind flies, by contrast, to loyal Odysseus, wistfully evoked by Agamemnon. Loyal Odysseus, going home to loyal Penelope who waits there, at the center of her web, weaving, endlessly weaving a faithful design. But Ithaca is another story. Here, a lover for Clytemnestra.

But Aegisthus does not accept a mere lover's role. Not at all! Justice! he cries. Justice at last! And he reveals himself as an avenging son. I am the third child, he proclaims, the infant who escaped! Agamemnon's father did terrible things to my father, and he killed my brothers. But I was overlooked. I grew up, I waited, I planned. They all forgot. Cassandra reminded them, warned them, but they ignored her. I did not forget. I remembered. Every day I remembered: my poor father who should have been king; my poor devoured brothers, their place usurped by Agamemnon and Menelaus. Every day I remembered the butchery, the usurpations, while the inheritors of wickedness, with convenient amnesia, forgot about justice and lived in palaces, dared to have wives, dared to have children, dared—those hypocrites—to wage "just" war. But I did not forget. And what of Agamemnon now? His wife is mine; his palace is mine; his city is mine. He took my place and now I stand in his. Justice at long last!

The intrusion of Aegisthus—we feel it as an intrusion—is deeply disconcerting. Our attention is fixed on Agamemnon and Clytemnestra, on their story, and suddenly we are jolted. Theirs is not the whole story. It is only part of a bigger story and, it begins to dawn on us, an endless one. There are earlier chapters; there are chapters still to come. The story is as long as memory. Remember Iphigenia; remember Atreus; remember (do you remember?) his father . . . remember Pearl Harbor; remember Lidice; remember Katyn; remember Jerusalem . . . . There is always someone brooding in the wings, someone who remembers what we have forgotten, what we want to forget, who does not share the general amnesia, who has not granted amnesty, for whom the happy ending is still to come.

Aegisthus destroys the comfortable boundaries of a self-contained present. There is a deeper past, still present, deeper roots quietly nourishing an unexpected crop. So, when Clytemnestra, her passion spent, says "Stop. Let's stop now. It is over. We're even. Enough. Let us have peace," we know how futile her prayer is. Iphigenia is dead. Electra is weeping in her room. But where is the third child? Where is Orestes? Somewhere, in exile, remorselessly growing, he remembers his father, the great Agamemnon, shamefully slain. He will never forget. Never! He will come home. It is too soon for peace. He will want justice.

II. THE LIBATION BEARERS

The king is dead. Who will mourn him? Who will, who can, conduct the funeral rites?

Never mind, Clytemnestra had answered coldly, it will be a private funeral.

What was there to say? We bury today the man who led us to victory in the great war. We have just killed him. Because the sacrifice was too great. Because it took so long. Because he neglected domestic affairs and the home front. Because of accumulated grievances, some a generation old. Because it was time for the peace party to take over. Because we want, we need, we are entitled to a new deal, peace and justice. If we mourn and praise him, why did we overthrow him? If we condemn him and rejoice—there is this sentimental mob. My king, my king, they mutter . . . . No. Better no state funeral.

There have been no last rites. Years have passed, but Agamemnon has not really been laid to rest. The queen has not been sleeping well. She decides to propitiate the dead. But she does not go to Agamemnon's grave herself. She sends her daughter, Electra, and the servants. What to say is still a problem.

We begin at the neglected grave. Orestes has secretly returned; he meets Electra with the belated procession. There is a recognition scene. The decision to kill Clytemnestra and Aegisthus is taken, confirmed, strengthened. The plot is carried out. Orestes kills Aegisthus. He kills his mother, Clytemnestra. Then, his mind in turmoil, he begins his long flight from the Furies.

•

It is a world of children. Of children and their servants, nurses, tutors, who complete their instruction before our eyes. They rehearse Electra in the grim catechism. How shall I pray, she asks. Pray for the murderers. What for? For revenge! Their every intervention is to provoke, remind, incite. They have skulked through the domestic corridors with their grievances and pass the treasure on to the children. So, it is the young and their teachers against the parental establishment. The eagle's brood, demi-orphaned, commune over the grave of their father. Young, aggrieved, bitter. A rotten family! An unjust world! They declare war.

The established order against which they war is the reign of Clytemnestra and Aegisthus, the post-war regime, cool to the glory of battle on the plains of Troy. Agamemnon has been overthrown. The righters of wrongs are in power. The queen seems to be in love with the new king (a satyr to Hyperion!). We do not hear of foreign expeditions. They go in for domestic improvements. Come, we have hot water, good beds, everything the weary traveler needs. The anguish is over, although the queen still has nightmares. Living is easier, even a bit lavish. It is odd how the servants grumble; they seem to miss the war. And Electra is unhappy, still unmarried. And Orestes . . . . There are some flaws, some loose ends. But they are doing a good job. They rule diligently, they make war no more, they shun sacrifice. We should get a proper sense of the situation, feel the pervasive righteousness of the life of the city. The rulers are not cruel. No one is groaning under the lash. If the servants, the people, miss the good old days it is nostalgia, not oppression. The old scores have been settled. There has been a revolution. Another does not seem necessary.

Another revolution, that is, may not seem necessary to the middle-aged who have been through the mill, who have endured the summoning of the hosts, the long war, the hazardous homecoming, the civil conflict, and who will gladly settle for the excitements of domesticity. But to the disinherited young, chanting over the untended grave of the hero-father, over his lost cause, the scene is less inviting.

How young are they? In their early twenties, I suppose, although as we watch them, side by side in their relentless ceremony of dedication at the grave, a few years melt away and they seem like fierce, pure, unforgiving teen-agers. Sometimes they seem to slip back more deeply into childhood. Hamlet is an adult, with an adult's reluctance and doubt. Orestes is still only a big boy. They are children in one of the archetypal soap operas: the husband who puts his career ahead of his family; the alienated wife who takes a lover and destroys her husband at his moment of triumph; the resentful daughter, left to sulk, who scorns her stepfather and dreams of her brother's return; the brother who returns, the bearer of hope, the bright young avenger . . . .

To children, the sins of parents threaten the very world, their home, the eternal present which, after the irreparable blow suddenly winds down to a desolate end. To the children of Agamemnon, it was mother's fault. She struck the fatal blow. They are on father's side. But he is dead; she is remarried; home is gone.

Next, wiping away those tears, they see themselves as heirs, as the inheritors, the succeeding generation. In this case, the dispossessed. Electra lives among the servants, a doubtful heiress. Orestes is tired of living on a shoestring abroad and wants to claim his father's property—his property—which *they* are enjoying. He will fight for what his father would want him to have. The inheritance, the property, the position, the power.

But he has also inherited a burden. Everywhere he goes it is the same story. Orestes? *The* Orestes? Tragic about your father. I was with him during the war. A great man . . . . What are your plans? Have you been to Delphi? Well, good luck in Argos! Everywhere, he meets the assessing gaze, the measuring look. Can he do it? Can he exact justice for his father? Can he bring Argos back into line? Can he serve the gods as his father did? There are intimations of political considerations of which he is only dimly aware: the fruits lost for lack of leadership . . . the dissipation of unity . . . Hellenic identity . . . the symbolic significance of the line of Atreus . . . . But whatever all that means, the first step is always justice for Agamemnon. Without that, nothing; beyond that, we will see.

So they stand there at the grave, protean shaped, changing as we watch them—now tearful children, now baffled heirs, now the ruthless bearers of a cause. They plan the deadly raid, the revenge, the revolution, the restoration.

There are some nice touches. Orestes and Pylades—his friend, fellow-traveler, mentor—lightly disguised, claim a place for the night. Clytemnestra, sensitive about hospitality (remember Zeus?) grants it with an open hand. Then she is tested. Orestes delivers the news that Orestes is dead. Oh God, she cries, that too? And she goes into the house. To weep? The old nurse enters. "She pretends she's sad, but she's really glad." Mean gossip. A babyish trick. She'll think I'm dead and then she'll be sorry!

Aegisthus, disarmed by a ruse and never much of a fighter anyway, is quickly killed. A servant rushes out. Bad news! The master is dead! He has a servant who thinks his death a bad thing. Strange!

And now Orestes is face to face with his mother. They have steeled him for this moment. When she says "my son!" you

40

are to cry "my father!" Of course, she says "my son . . . "
Orestes falters. What should I do Pylades? Should I kill my
mom? Pylades, his moment come, keeps his head. Go ahead.
You promised . . . .

The final argument is a child railing at his mother who
knows, hopelessly, that she cannot really explain, that he is
incapable of understanding, that there is nothing she can do,
or really cares to do, about it. Get me an axe, quick, she had
called earlier. But it doesn't arrive. Or if it has, she is not going
to use it. Her good husband, the only real happiness of her
life, lies dead. Her strangely grown son, deranged, feverish,
gesticulates wildly, babbling accusations. You sent me away!
You didn't care. What about daddy? If you love *him* so much
I'll bury you together so you can sleep with him all the time!

She interjects hopelessly—some things had to be done . . . it
was for your own good . . . you don't understand about
love . . . killing your mother won't make you happy . . . . But
she gives up. Children!

Her last thoughts would be worth knowing. Does it all pass
quickly through her mind? Her childhood: the sleepy pond,
the swans; growing up with sister Helen; the marriages, young
queen and mother in Argos; Agamemnon's growing
restlessness, the glint of Atrean madness in his eyes; the world-
shattering sacrifice, the long, long war; the comfort of
Aegisthus, poor gentle victim; their plot, the killing of the
blood-soaked father of her children; the slow struggle to build
a better world in peace, with love. And now finally, Orestes,
poor child, thinking I didn't recognize him in his outlandish
costume, unmistakable, his father's look in his eyes, now
leading me to my husband's corpse for my final exit. Poor
Orestes. How I will haunt him . . . .

But it is not merely a family story. There is a persistent
Olympian interest in what goes on. Some vindication of
Agamemnon is called for. The repudiation of him, of his war,
of his policy is not to be the last word. He was assassinated,
and there is the matter of justice. What we have just seen is
not simply the killing of a husband and wife. It is the overthrow
of a king and a queen, a regime. Nevertheless, the domestic

note dominates, and it does so because the crusade for justice is, in this stage, a children's crusade. Children's eyes peer at a world that seems to have no place for them. The power structure they know is parental, although faithless and murderous. The children will set right what they so clearly know to be wrong. Their generation will replace the corrupt adults. I will be better than my mother, vows Electra.

They see clearly, but not far enough. They have not yet absorbed the cultural memory. They see the sins of Clytemnestra and Aegisthus. They do not remember them as sinned against. Orestes does not realize that Aegisthus is an earlier Orestes. He does not discuss anything with Aegisthus; he does not listen to his mother. It would have been too confusing, too complicated. He might have hesitated, he might not have acted decisively. There would have been no progress. He had to act before he listened, before he became corrupted by understanding.

Orestes is unlucky. Not every struggle for justice must begin at home. Nor, if it does, must we take it so literally. In his case it does begin at home; it begins with matricide. His bad luck is the kind that seems to run in the family; his father had it too. They have no margin of metaphoric fat to live on. Agamemnon sacrifices his daughter. Sacrifices? Neglects? Spends too little time playing with her? Forgets her birthday? Skimps on her education? No, no. Sacrifice! With a knife! Orestes fights with his mother? To the hilt! A real hilt! They have the bad luck of the archetype. Metaphor is a luxury.

Orestes displays the bodies of Aegisthus and Clytemnestra and launches into a speech of justification. As he speaks something happens to him; he grows incoherent, he begins to see things. The abetting chorus thinks he is a bit hysterical—understandably, still covered with blood. He announces that he will go to Apollo, to Delphi, to the inspiration of his mission to straighten everything out. He is very upset about his mother. He thinks he is losing his mind.

But he is not losing his mind. He is coming to his senses. The madness was earlier when, in the grip of things he did not understand, he moved through the paces of his childish plot. That was when he was out of his mind. His was the familiar madness of the person in the grip of a gleaming simple idea, who *does* it, who believes the theory, who takes it literally, to whom horrible things seem right to do.

What does he begin to realize as he looks at his bloody hands? That he is the latest in a line of murderers? Does he remember what his tutors have dinned into him—blood calls for blood, the killer must be killed? Does he, looking in a daze at the applauding chorus have a chilling premonition? Who are these old women, nodding, so pleased, so bloodthirsty? Nice nannies, sweet old ladies? Then why, behind the smile, does he glimpse the edge of a hungry grin? Why do the toil-worn hands hover like talons? The crones are shaking their heads, dank hair snakelike in disarray. They are still saying "brave boy, well done!" But they glance covertly at each other. They lick their lips. There is a growing murmur. His mother . . . he really did it . . . his own mother, after all . . . horrible . . . unforgivable . . . he won't hear the last of this . . . with his own hands . . . .

No, the madness is going. Orestes is coming to his senses. He flees.

III. THE EUMENIDES

Guilt and indignation, spurred by the memory of Clytemnestra, pursue Orestes. Finally, at Athens, the problem is faced and resolved. The Furies, representing the principles of retribution, of justice, are subordinated to something new. Orestes escapes the Furies. But not through the operation of love, or mercy, or a higher morality. He is not forgiven; he is tried and acquitted. Moral fervor is supplanted by legality. Justice gives way to law. Fury is brought under constraint. From now on, we are to go to court. It is a turning point in the history of civilization.

•

We have seen a succession of outrages. A father kills his

daughter; a wife kills her husband; a son kills his mother. But "kills" does not tell us enough; we need more information. A father sacrifices his daughter; the wife avenges her daughter by killing her husband; the son avenges his father by killing his mother. More? The great leader, heartsick, saves the "cause" by making the necessary sacrifice of his beloved daughter . . . .

As we add, characterize, describe, our judgment falters. We begin to understand, to defend, to excuse. But not always in the same way. If we brood sympathetically over Agamemnon, seeing him as summoned to lead a holy war that will forge a great people, surmounting the test of personal sacrifice, akin, in some degree, to Moses and Abraham, then his death at the hands of his disloyal vindictive wife may seem, indeed, an outrage. He is the hero; she the low betrayer. But if life has taught us that all war is folly, that no war is just or holy, that Olympus is always an illusion or a license for fanatics, what must we think of Agamemnon then? A fool, a ruthless monster, a destroyer of the innocent, a grim tyrant fortunately cut down—a pity it wasn't sooner—in mid-career by his long-suffering, desperate wife. She saves the city by netting and slaying the beast as he returns to his lair.

Which is the right account? On this question, we will always have Agamemnonites and Clytemnestrans. It would be nice if the issues were clearer. But good and evil are not unambiguously labelled. If they seem to be, it is a defect in perception. Beyond, behind the question of whether good will triumph over evil lies a more terrible question. Who is in the right? Which is evil? Moral confusion is the setting for the moral struggle. We begin with some degree of moral chaos.

It is not a chaos in which the moral categories have no place, in which there is no notion of right or wrong. It is not an amoral, booming, buzzing confusion. It is more like the real human world. Judgments of right and wrong cry out to be made. We accuse or defend Agamemnon, Clytemnestra, Aegisthus, Orestes. But we do not agree. Even the higher powers disagree; principles clash. To Apollo, Orestes acted rightly in executing his father's murderer; to the Furies, Orestes acted immorally in killing his mother. The disagreement is fundamental, impervious to persuasion. Conflicting judgments are not, because of the conflict, diffident or uncertain. They are confident and irreconcilable. In a remote spectator the clash of views might generate a baffled skepticism. But on the field of battle, contradiction does not generate self-doubt. It merely identifies the enemy.

We live, then, in a turmoil of diverging moral judgment. The human sense of rightness does not speak with a single voice. What I may condone you may find abominable. We are not moved to the same indignation. We disagree about who is right; or rather, each is sure that he is right.

The world of moral conflict is not made up of discrete bits spread out before us, of separate actions, each complete in itself, but rather of chains, of actions essentially linked to each other. "Orestes killed Clytemnestra" is not the significant unit of understanding. Orestes killed Clytemnestra who murdered Agamemnon who sacrificed Iphigenia so that he could destroy Troy which sheltered Paris who stole Helen . . . . The quality of a link depends upon its place in the sequence. The current event is only part of the story.

The series or chain may extend across generations. Consequently, the significant unit may not be the single or solitary person but a more complex unit—a family, a city, a people. Debts may be incurred by families and bills presented to the hapless sons of profligate fathers. The innocent son lives a blameless life on the family estate, on the ill-gotten gains of his rapacious father. Can he keep the family estate and wash his hands of his father's sins? I didn't do it, Agamemnon might have said to Aegisthus, my father did it to your father; I inherit the fruits but not the guilt. But in a world in which we inherit property, benefit, status, and advantage, is it so clear that we do not also inherit blame, responsibility? May not moral books be kept and balanced across generational lines? Morally, responsibility for what one may not have done himself complicates the world, but it may not be altogether absurd.

Finally, there is, in this confused, tangled world no clear center of certainty and authority. We consult different oracles inspired by different gods. Apollo does not speak for, has no authority over, the Furies, the daughters of night. There is no single ultimate authority, no unanswerable final voice. This is the familiar world upon which the *Eumenides* opens.

Orestes is trying to escape justice. That, at least, is how the Furies would put it. They pursue him because he has done a horrible thing. He has slaughtered his mother. If there is justice in the world he will pay for what he has done. And, they affirm, there is justice in the world. They are there, the handmaids of justice, to see that the wrong-doer, the murderer, the matricide, gets what he deserves. And what is justice but the principle of deservedness, that we are done by as we do, that the moral books be brought into balance, that the evil do not escape retribution?

Justice is not a bloodless principle. There is a point about fury. Justice is based in outrage. Deeply rooted in a normal social creature is the instinctive passionate response to action that violates or threatens the integrity of social life. The perception of injustice unleashes fury. When others do evil, we seethe with indignation; when we do evil, we are devoured by guilt. Without these, without indignation and guilt, no social unit would endure; without these, we are less than human.

Orestes is human. He has been pursued by indignation and tormented by guilt. But time passes. He has behaved himself for quite a while. The blood has been washed from his hands and he wears a clean shirt. The pangs of guilt have subsided. He was, it now seems clear to him, only following Apollo's orders. Indignation, even, flags and slumbers until spurred by a reviving memory. Orestes? *The* Orestes . . . . No, even now, the case is not closed. The Furies still pursue him. They are uncompromising, unforgiving.

There is something odd about the Furies. They claim to be, and the claim is never challenged, the agents of justice. They are the avengers, the bane of evil. But they are described as loathsome, disgusting, revolting, ugly. Why? Is not justice a good thing? Do we not revere it? Does it not have a terrible beauty? So wherefore loathsome? Why do we shudder at the sight of justice?

We will say, of course, that it is not justice itself that is ugly but the pursuit of justice, the means, the instruments, that add up to an ugly business. How could it be otherwise? We are dealing with transgressors. We are not awarding prizes. We are doling out suffering to those who cause suffering, to those who deserve to suffer, to those who, if they are not seen to suffer, outrage our sense that this is a just world. The world of retribution is, in principle, a world of pain; it is ruled by fear, not by love. The Furies claim that no city that is free of fear will care much about justice, that the fear of punishment is indispensable for peace and good order. If we need fear, something must be grim, terrifying. So, the agents, the instruments must make us shudder. But they serve a bright, a noble end.

A noble end? A great intrinsic good? Why do we think that? Why, when we think about retribution, about paying and paying back, do we consider it as anything but a sad necessity, at best a necessary evil? Is there not something depressing, hollow, about justice achieved? Is not deservedness a rather thin spiritual diet? The nice gods don't seem to care much about justice. Apollo scorns the Furies. And some of our nicest people seem to agree with him. Justice involves punishment. And the desire to punish is seen as an expression of our baser nature. What good does it do? Does it cure? Does it deter? Merely to satisfy our retributive rage? Merely to see Nixon suffer? (more! more!). Do good people have such barbaric feelings? We blush at our secret pleasure.

As we see the Furies in relentless pursuit of Orestes let us quickly review what we believe in. We believe in treatment. We believe in mercy. We believe in love. We believe that it is really society's fault. Perhaps we believe in justice, but it is an ugly business. We are ready to contribute to the fund for the defense of Orestes. Too bad about the victim, of course, but what do you want? An eye for an eye? A pound of flesh? What good will it do? The diligent handmaids of justice have become the villains of the piece. How will Orestes escape?

The great creative solution unfolds before us. Athena establishes a court to hear the case. There will be a jury of twelve citizens. What the court decides goes. In case of a tie,

Athena will cast a vote to break the tie. It is a new idea.

The argument over Orestes had reached a dead end. The Furies asserted that he had killed his mother and must be punished. Apollo asserted that Orestes had properly killed Clytemnestra in order to avenge Agamemnon. But he killed his mother! But he avenged his father! He killed a parent! She had killed a spouse! Which outweighs which? Neither side gives way. But the defense now comes in with a surprise. You charge Orestes with killing his parent? But he did not kill his parent. He only killed his mother. The father is the parent; he plants the child in the mother, the garden. A mother isn't even necessary. Behold Athena herself, who sprang, like a bright idea, from Zeus, her father's head! Orestes is, therefore, not guilty of the charge of killing his parent!

The jury is evenly divided and Athena is called upon to settle the matter. She makes a charming, uncomplicated speech which pierces to the heart of the matter. I have no mother. I always side with the men. So I vote for Orestes. He is acquitted. He can go.

The winning legal argument is wonderfully ludicrous. It foreshadows centuries of legal antics. But what should we expect? That the legal argument would be better, higher, more profound than the moral argument that had reached an impasse? The moral argument had already expressed the intuitive insights and presented all the reasonable excuses. We are not going to be rescued from moral chaos by a new moral insight. The legal argument, if we are to escape through that, is bound to be less compelling. It does not provide illumination; it provides an escape. It is technical. It is foolish. It is not worth taking seriously. But it helps us escape justice. It saves Orestes from the Furies.

As usual, deeper, persistent issues swirl about the test case. It is more than just Orestes. There is, to begin with, the long-running fight between the new (the young) and the old; between progressive and conservative. The Furies accuse the young gods, the upstart Olympians, of lack of respect for the ancient verities. Apollo considers the Furies old-fashioned, passé. Punishment, retribution, vengeance are valued only by the unenlightened. The newer Apollonian consciousness turns with contempt and with a shudder from the calculus of pain, from all the ways in which the vindictive mind seeks to administer the just dessert. It disdains the hard-line law-and-order mentality and its cynical view of human nature. The Furies are primeval. Apollo is a liberal. Apollo wins this skirmish, but the war is still on.

Then, there is the battle between the sexes. The Furies are female. Clytemnestra is their issue—the mother, the woman. They care about the family, about blood ties. The women are rather fierce. Clytemnestra and Electra are unforgiving. They are not numbered among the meek. At this stage, they seem to be losing out. At this stage, the liberals are committed to male supremacy. The Orestes case is a set-back for mothers.

There is also the conflict between the familial and the civic, between the family and broader associations. And it is the progressive male who is seen as transcending the limitations of the family, as becoming more political and less paternal—as Agamemnon became when he sacrificed his daughter for the cause and became the effective leader of the Greeks, not merely the head of the house of Atreus.

Old and new, progressive and conservative, male and female, family and state—all these persistent dualities come to a focus on the fate of Orestes. His acquittal is a minor matter, and partisan triumph is transient. But what is really, enduringly, important is the dual achievement of Athena: the imposition of legality upon the world of moral chaos; and the settlement with the Furies.

Moral chaos does not blend into peace; it breeds war. When there is nothing to do but follow our own views about what is right, when there is nothing to which our conscience must defer, our situation is precarious. How can we resolve the inevitable conflict? Persuasion? That snare of innocence? Force? Does might make right? Athena finds the answer. Moral intuition must subject itself to institutional legal judgment. We must authorize a court to settle the matter. It will be human. It will not be terribly wise. But we are to accept its decree. The Athenian settlement is a bit unexpected. Appeal to Athena, Apollo had told Orestes. Well, we think, she represents wisdom. She will listen. And then she will say, Aha! Don't you see, she will say . . . and then we will say, Of course! How obvious . . . .

And it will all be settled the right way. But she does not do that. She is too wise. It is a tough question, she says, and there are gods on both sides. We'd better have a jury. . . . It is like Alexander the Great at Gordium. They invite him to untangle the knotted mess. He cuts through it. So Athena, in her wisdom, proposes to subject the moral tangle to the rule of law.

But Athena knows that she must come to terms with the baffled Furies. They must be appeased, not defied. She recognizes that if the fundamental, even primitive, sense of justice is flouted, peace is impossible; that thwarted indignation brews a deadly venom. The legal order must respect moral intuition; it must express it; it must satisfy it. It cannot do so perfectly. There is no moral consensus about Orestes. Someone may feel outraged or betrayed by whatever the court does. But the court, the law, cannot go its way indifferent to the Furies. The law must claim, and try, to serve justice. If it strays too far the Furies will be stirred to a vigilante rampage. Justice may be stretched a bit, but it cannot be mocked or parodied with impunity. The final symbolism is striking. Athena gives the Furies a new home in a cave under the courthouse. Fury is suppressed; it goes underground; it lives at the foundation of the court; it supports the law. Law rests on traditional morality. It must try not to reawaken the Furies that doze in the subterranean depths.

More radical solutions are not adopted. The new order does not break with retributive order in pursuit of purely utilitarian aims. It does not hail mercy and love as supplanting mere justice. No. Law, the civic-political order, is set above the moral chaos of the state of nature. This, I think, is the ultimate point of the Orestes case. The theme is the taming of the Furies, the institutionalization of moral indignation, salvation through the law.

•

Civilization requires the taming of the passions. The Trojan War was about the curbing of Aphrodite, the subordination of love to domesticity. The *Oresteia* is about the taming of the other great passion, moral fury. Law does for morality what marriage does for love. It gives it an endurable form. The solitary figure of Agamemnon looms in legend at the crucial point of the double taming. As the heroic leader he restored Helen; love's darling, to her husband and home. As his own wife's victim, his cause brought Orestes to Athena. Agamemnon's final vindication is the taming of the Furies.

•

Agamemnon:
This is, on the whole, a more sympathetic account than I have come to expect. Homer's story of my quarrel with Achilles—to be perfectly frank, my mishandling of Achilles—has made it seem that Troy was conquered in spite of me. But the author skips my military record, so it would be inappropriate to try to set that straight here.

I agree, of course, that the war was just and necessary. I was prepared to insist on it, but I see that I don't have to. Trade routes! Loot! Glory! No doubt. But believe me, I would not have offered up Iphigenia for *that*. We were fighting for the glory that was to be Greece, and for Western civilization. I take what the author calls the Olympian view, although I'm not sure I understand what he says about the institutionalization of the libido. You should have seen Priam's palace. Fortunately, a basic monogamy, with its supplementary institutions, prevailed. No, if we had not sailed against Troy you would not have heard of Greece or Rome or New York (I speak now from a timeless perspective). We had to go.

Even now, I can hardly bear to think about the sacrifice. It was the most difficult thing I ever had to do. I wonder what would have happened if Artemis had held up the second front in World War II. Stalin would have done it. Churchill? Roosevelt? Truman? They all had daughters . . . . A world is poised for the assault on Hitler, and the word filters back—it's off, he won't do it. All those ships, all those planes, all those armies—thousands ready to die for the cause. But the leader won't give the word. He can sacrifice you, but not *her*. No. I had to do it. I did it. Afterwards, no one ever mentioned it, not in my hearing. It made me seem awful or awesome, and it certainly

51

made my leadership unchallengeable.

Do I think the Artemis ceremony a good thing? I suppose you mean, would it prevent unnecessary wars. I don't know. Abstractly, it seems like a good idea. But it might result only in our having more ruthless leaders, screen out the more decent ones. And, let me say from personal experience, once the leader has made the sacrifice he is not going to put up with any nonsense about reducing casualties . . . after that, the gloves are off.

I don't think I want to comment about Clytemnestra. Whatever I say about her gets twisted into some sort of criticism. Let her tell her own side of it.

I never did meet Aegisthus. A cousin on my father's side. What can I say? It's ridiculous to be blamed for something you didn't do. The sins of the fathers should stop right there. These new courts are criticized, but one thing they do right—they don't care about ancient history. What did the accused do? Period! I don't consider myself responsible for my father. You know, I suppose that Aegisthus's father seduced my father's wife, my mother, that is. But there's no point to rehashing all that. It's irrelevant. What did *I* do, that's the question. I'm ready to answer for that. Yes, I inherited the "ill-gotten gains," if that's what they were—let's not beg that question—but that's just a matter of luck, and since when is luck supposed to be fair. For that matter, was it fair to duck out of the war, to hang around and seduce my wife while I was overseas? You were more than fair to Aegisthus.

Ah, yes. Orestes. I hardly knew him. A strange lad. Of course I appreciate what he did for me. All the same, a strange young man.

•

Clytemnestra:
By the time the war ended I had very little choice. Of course, Iphigenia was the turning point. I was not blind to Agamemnon's problem, but I could not forgive him. It was then I acknowledged that I no longer loved my husband. But ten years is a long time, and if nothing else had happened I don't

think I would have killed him. Something else did happen. Nothing sudden or dramatic. I felt alienated, bitter, lonely and in growing sympathy with the anti-war movement. Then Aegisthus appeared. Gradually, eventually, we fell in love, irrevocably. So Agamemnon's return posed a problem that had outgrown Iphigenia. There was no other way out. Of course it was an early warning system I set up. We could have waited for the joy of victory, but we needed time to prepare the reception. We had to act immediately, before he could find out about us. So it was not just Iphigenia. By that time, it was self-defense.

I can't justify killing Cassandra. It wasn't necessary. I don't know why I did it.

I agree that I was more domestic than political. And not thrilled by paradox. Sacrificing a child in order to vindicate the family; destroying a city full of homes for the sake of the sanctity of the home—I refuse to understand these political profundities. Stay home and practice the traditional morality. Then there would be fewer courts talking masculine nonsense like "a mother is not a parent."

Ah, yes. Orestes. A strange boy. Perhaps I should have kept him at home. I thought it was too risky. It was one of those decisions. Poor boy! I still think of him as "poor boy." It doesn't matter what the court said. I think he knows what he did. And to whom.

•

Orestes:
What is all this "strange lad," "poor boy" nonsense. I will not be treated as a child! And I do not need to be forgiven. I was acquitted.

•

Athena:
Your prayer was heard. But we never explain.

53

"O Lear, Lear, Lear!"

Then isn't one supposed, in common humanity, and if one hasn't quarreled with him, and one has the means, and he, on his side doesn't kick up rows—isn't one supposed to keep one's aged parent in one's life?

—*The Golden Bowl,* Henry James

Part One

King Lear is a warning against unraveling the garment of ceremony and custom that stands between us and the storm of raw nature. Civilization is ceremony. We are to see what happens when, through romantic folly, we expose ourselves to the unceremonious world.

GONERIL

Father was full of surprises that day. In the morning I was the conventional eldest daughter, the Duchess of Albany, a bit bored with waiting but expecting that my husband would eventually succeed Father as king and that I would then provide the backbone for my easy-going mate and, in fact, rule the kingdom. By evening it was a different world. Father had flown into a rage, had entered, rather, the state of rage from which he was only intermittently to emerge; Cordelia had been disowned and led away, without dowry, by the silly King of France; the kingdom was split in two and my husband got only half—the half a crown that is no better than none—insuring, of course, a civil war; Father announced that he would be our guest for a month, and alternate months after that, with an entourage of a hundred knights; and I was launched on my notorious career. I was to become the ungrateful monster who drove her generous old father out into the cruel world. I was to fall in love with a handsome, ambitious bastard, become an adulteress, plot to kill my husband, poison my foolishly competitive sister, and then, when my lover was killed, commit suicide. But I suppose Father meant well.

He was in one of his cheerful moods—decisions made and about to dash off to hunt—and he announced briskly to the assembled court that he was going to retire, that he was dividing the kingdom into three parts, and that he was finally going to settle the question of Cordelia's marriage. That was quite a list, and I was stunned. Retire? So he could do "an unburdened crawl to death"? Nonsense! A dashing crawl on horseback! No, they had finally convinced him. Give youth a chance. Why should the young have to wait so long in the wings? Turn things over to a fresh generation. Bow out gracefully, don't cling, don't make them push—the whole stale litany of impatience. And the equal division of the kingdom! That, too, God help us, "to forestall future strife." And he is finally letting his Cordelia go?

There was, of course, no chance to protest, no time to argue, no time to think. Father rushed on. He was playing our old childhood game—"now girls," his hands hiding baubles behind his back, "let's see who loves me most . . ." I managed (I don't think I showed how upset I was) to recite a version of my "more than words can say" speech, and Father promptly handed over a third of the kingdom. I even managed a smile as he blithely robbed me of two-thirds of what was to have been mine.

"And now Regan . . ." I must explain a little about sister Regan. We are alike in many ways. She is less intelligent than I am but makes up for it by being more ruthless. She is terribly ambitious (as is her husband, the Duke of Cornwall) and does not defer happily to my seniority. And now Regan makes her speech. Typical. "I say what Goneril says, only more!" And gets her present, a third of my kingdom.

"And now, Cordelia . . ." I had noticed that Cordelia was sulking and muttering, so I was not altogether surprised when she refused to play. She used to play the game quite well, but that was before she grew up. Now she scorns games, ceremonies, rituals. She is having a prolonged attack of sincerity. She believes in being natural, simple, truthful. That is, she now despises her sisters who put on make-up, wear masks, say the expected right things, keep their feelings from showing, respect the proprieties, have good manners, observe the forms, present an outward appearance that does not fully reflect the inner state, who are not, in short, entirely what they seem. Cordelia has recently discovered the gap between appearance and reality, between the ceremonial and the natural, if not yet between outer grace and inner darkness. We are to her, to put it without ceremony, hypocrites, and she won't play our lying games. She could have said, "Father, I love you even more than my sisters do," and it might have been true as well as simple and honest and all the things she believes in. But no, that would have been *too* simple. She had to demonstrate that she didn't inhabit the same moral universe as her sisters, so she simply refused to play the game. She said "nothing" and, as everyone says these days, nothing will come of nothing.

Father was incredulous, embarrassed, hurt, shocked. It is hard to believe, I cannot believe, that it suddenly dawned on him that she didn't love him. He was chagrined at the unseemly breakdown of the ceremony of gratitude, at the public display of bad manners, of undisciplined moral eccentricity. He must have seen in that moment of revelation that he had neglected the education of his favorite, that he had been too indulgent in allowing her to remain a romantic child flitting around chanting "the king is naked!"—her favorite story, naturally—

long after the line had lost its novelty and its childish point. There she was, with ostentatious artlessness, exposing sham. "Why do my sisters have husbands if they say they love you all?" It was a painful display of childish malice. Father did not let it pass. He exploded in rage, and when the dust had settled Cordelia was gone and the kingdom was now divided into two parts.

Regan and I held a hasty consultation about Father's condition, the problems it would pose for us, and agreed that something would have to be done about it. Still, I remember thinking, what Father does in a sudden rage is not as bad as what he does when he has time to make plans.

He was, as expected, an impossible guest. He descended on us with his hundred knights in an uproarious invasion. Father insisted, when I finally put my foot down, that they were all perfect gentlemen and behaved impeccably. I may have exaggerated when I said they had turned my home into a cross between a tavern and brothel, but it was bad enough. It was not only the tumult; Father was having severe identity problems. He stopped my faithful steward, Oswald, to complain about a falling-off (at my orders) of the service. "Sir," Father demanded, "who am I?" "My lady's father," Oswald replied. And Father beat him.

Was it the wrong answer? Who, what did he think he was? The king? No, he was not the king. He was the retired king, the former king. He had given up the power, the responsibility, the ruling function. He wanted to cling to the appearance, but the appearance, the show, the entourage, led him to deceive himself. He still, as someone said, had the look of authority, and he would describe himself as "every inch a king," but he was not the king. There is a lesson here, but he had not learned it: if you are not king until you die, you must die to being king. "Who am I?" He beat Oswald for trying to make him face the truth. In my house, he was only my father. My father, but not even the father, the head, of the house. He didn't realize that either.

Why don't we say former father as we say former king? I am a former child, am I not? For every former child there is, if still lingering after the task is done, a former parent. The parental role must be relinquished; it is not a permanent one; the function has a stop. Oswald should have said "my lady's one-time father." Poor Lear, as I should call him, was quite lost. No more kinging; no more parenting; only the habit of commanding and the expectation of deference.

When I had had enough, he began on gratitude. "I gave you every thing!" I did not bother to point out that he had halved my rightful expectations without even a courtesy consultation. "Is this the thanks I get?" I thanked you very nicely, don't you remember, I replied. "And is this how you repay me?" Repay you? Repay? But you said it was a gift! Father—I see I must still call him Father—stared dumbfounded. In the end he stormed off, more generous with his curses than with his blessings, to sample Regan's gratitude.

I do believe in showing respect for parents, even for former parents, and I had not really intended to drive him away, but his leaving was a not unwelcome relief. It freed me to begin to clear up the mess left by his abdication. Nothing may come from nothing, but everything rushes to fill a vacuum. He had created one, and the scramble was on. I did not mean to lose out, not only because I had the best claim to inherit but also, speaking objectively, because I had the only responsible political mind on the scene. War was afoot. The old guard, those who had had it very well under Father, suddenly cast adrift and expecting cold comfort from me or Regan, were already plotting a "restoration," hoping for France to invade in the name of Cordelia and Old Lear, suddenly seen, through tears, as poor victims of injustice. We, Regan and I, Cornwall and Albany, needed to unite against the foreign invasion and against the traitorous uprising that would support it. After that there would be a showdown between Cornwall and Albany. In that final struggle the support of Gloster would be crucial. The old earl would be loyal to Father; that is, he would be a traitor siding with France. He must be supplanted.

By Edmund. Edmund was Gloster's illegitimate son, a man of great ability, charm, ambition—nature's nobleman, in short. He was, in the rapidly shifting political situation, maneuvering himself into the position left open by the treachery of his father. We were made for each other, and we had fallen in love. Our plan was to get rid of my husband, Albany, somehow. Then I would marry Edmund and we would make a run for the crown. When Cornwall was absurdly killed, Regan had an idea of her own. She would take Edmund as her husband (I said she wanted anything I wanted), make him Duke of Cornwall and, since Albany was really unfit for rough politics, Regan would end up as queen, with Edmund as her king. It was a practical plan, and I found it unbearable from every point of view. So I had to poison Regan. I won't bore you with the tale of my misfortunes. Albany got wind of my love and my plans, Edmund was killed by his legitimate brother, and I had nothing left to live for. My last thought before I died was, to my surprise, that I cared about Edmund more than about anything else, that this was really a love story.

EDMUND

I would have preferred to feel nothing but scorn for the ceremonial array that had a place in it for everyone but me, but instead I stood transfixed, slowly drowning in a wave of loneliness—solitary, forlorn, apart, outside, placeless, unbelonging. It was, I recognized, the loneliness of the bastard in the precincts of legitimacy. It is hard, impossible, for those who can take their legitimacy for granted, as something they are born to and never have to think about, to imagine what it is like to be born an outsider, marked from birth as illicit, a permanent jest about the consequences of sport, always braced for banter. I am too sensitive about it, I am told. "We don't think about it all the time." No, they don't think about it all the time. But we do. The view from the outside has an unavoidable awareness of edges.

I had been away for nine years, getting an education and seeing the world, and I had expected to find things here a bit rustic and rundown. But the court was gracefully impressive, the very height of civic order, the lost city haunting my dreams, and I fell bitterly in love with it. I would not leave if I could help it.

And then, unbelievably, the facade cracked, and the players on stage who, only a moment before, were moving through a stately dance, broke into insane capers. When the scene had ended I realized two things: that even here the appearance of order concealed pervasive chaos; and that it would be possible, taking advantage of that chaos, to win a place inside for myself. I also felt, slightly disenchanted, that while it would be easier to break in, the victory would be less rewarding than I had earlier hoped.

That the king should want to retire was hard to believe. He was still full of vigor. Was there something better than being king, than dying with the crown on? That the precious symbol of unity was proposing to split itself into three parts was even more unbelievable. Was he bored with peace? If everyone had suddenly laughed and applaud, as at a familiar court joke, I would, relieved, have joined in the laughter. But it was no joke.

And then—Goneril, say thank you! Thank you, sir. Regan, say thank you! Thank you, sir. Cordelia, say thank you! I won't! The rest is legend . . . .

I remember making two pledges: "Thou, Nature, art my Goddess; to thy law my services are bound"; and later, to Goneril, "Yours in the ranks of death." I kept both promises.

About nature. Since I first realized I was a merely natural son, I have been a confirmed civilization-watcher, a student of culture, custom, manners, rites, ceremony, form—of all that stands opposed, as human convention, to mere nature. It is an ancient distinction and I, with the sharpened perception of the eternal alien, am always aware of the wild edge of the human clearing. Children of the city, for whom nature is what you find in gardens, think the whole world is a civic order. They do not realize that the city is only a clearing in the jungle, that its writ does not run beyond its limits, that our local legitimacies mean nothing to the beasts out there and buried deep within us. So when I see a lovely court I marvel and I tremble for it. I am nature's child, but I do not love nature. I love the masterpiece of human craft, the beauty and order of a crown. Step softly, softly, cradle its fragility, preserve, protect, cherish. I come to worship, not to destroy. I am not an anarchist out to shatter the exclusive order to which I am bastard. I am rather, in intention, a usurper. I seek a place that is not mine. I crave legitimacy. I want in. But until I am legitimatized, fully admitted to the life of their laws, I must live by the deeper rules, by the law of nature. I am fully justified; I have done nothing wrong; I did not declare myself an outlaw. I was born unceremoniously, but it was my chortling father who skipped the ceremony, not I. They deny me a place in their system, in their game. They should not expect me to follow their rules. So I will live, until I am in, by the natural rules—"by whatever means necessary," as they say. And I will use my natural assets—the outsider's sharpened wits (man is by nature cunning), and the outsider's special way with the daughters of the establishment. I mean to win by wit what I am denied by birth.

Does this explain why I was so shocked by Lear and Cordelia? I saw Lear as committing an act of sacrilege against the great ceremony that was the crown—splitting it up and tossing it away. Cordelia was flaunting, in the name of sincerity, her contempt for the discipline of manners that checks and channels the wild flood of feeling. They were, together, being disastrously unconventional. They were bowing before the great romantic trinity—youth, equality, sincerity—breeders of chaos. Under that aegis no wonder communication failed, rage towered, the war between generations flared anew, and siblings renewed their rivalry. And I found my opening . . . .

My immediate objective was to take the place of my legitimate brother, to displace him. I must that is, steal my father's blessing and my brother's birthright. I used deception. Odd how history repeats itself. At one point my befuddled father actually said, "Is this Edgar's hand?" The ancient sentence floated into my mind. "The hands are the hands of Esau, but the voice is Jacob's." Like Jacob, I was a deceiver; like Jacob, I was engaged to two sisters; unlike Jacob, my brother did not forgive me, but I have little to complain of on that score.

I not only deceived my father, I betrayed him. He made a political blunder in siding with the old king and the French in the war, and Cornwall punished the poor old man as a

traitor—sending me away so I wouldn't have to witness it—
and made me Earl of Gloster in his place.

When war is unleashed, life turns on absurdities. The great
Duke of Cornwall is killed by an old servant—as if to proclaim
the natural equality of creatures before the sword. In turn, the
Duchess of Cornwall stabs the servant in the back. She is now
a widow and free to marry me, make me duke and beyond
that, she dreams king. I do not say no. But Goneril and I have
become lovers, hatching vain empires, it turns out, in the dark.
We are to get rid of her husband, and she will make me Duke
of Albany, and beyond that, king . . . . Almost, almost, but
nothing worked out. I was fatally wounded in a duel with my
brother. I had mixed feelings when I saw it was Edgar who
had beaten me. His legitimacy was not his fault and he had
always been decent to me. I would not have guessed he would
be so fine a swordsman. I had forgotten that the sons of the
established order go to the best schools and have the best of
fencing masters.

I was responsible for Cordelia's death. It was a purely
political move and when politics and ambition and everything
else was ending for me I tried to stop her execution, but it was
too late. I don't think she would have been happy had she lived.
She wasn't the happy type. I did not like Cordelia.

When my death was announced to Albany who was left to
pick up the pieces of the world shattered by Lear's folly, he
shrugged and said "That's but a trifle here."

Enter without ceremony . . . . Exit without ceremony . . . .

FROM THE FOOL'S NOTEBOOK

Stages in Lear's pilgrimage: Unkinged, he leaves the political
world; defathered, changed back into a child, he runs away
from home and enters, beyond the palace and the domicile,
the tempestuous natural world. Accompanied by Kent,
disguised as a servant, Edgar, disguised as a madman, and me,
disguised as a fool—man's basic expeditionary force.

•

Not like Circe. She turned men into beasts. See Lear as an old magician who has cast a spell turning beasts into humans, creating a splendid kingdom out of a collection of animals. They behave with courtly formality, go through all the human paces. But the magician, grown careless, tries his powers too far, expects too much. His pet, his favorite, breaks the spell. "It's all a fake," she pouts, "It's just a stupid game; I won't play!" The enraged magician, power lost, storms and curses to no avail. Illusions fade, creatures revert, and we are transported from a world in which music ushers in the very paragon of majesty to a world in which a tempest cues the entrance of a pathetic, aged, forked animal tormented by the forces he can no longer master.

•

Or an animal trainer and his traveling circus . . . .

•

No, not a magician, not an animal trainer. Avoid dramatic exaggeration; tone everything down from the extraordinary to the banal. Father decides to retire. Expects to enjoy his family. But children are grown up, married, preoccupied with husbands' careers. Father, hurt and rejected storms out of daughter's home. Finds shelter in a hovel in a rough neighborhood with a few odd companions. Children, on their own, come to a bad end. Father bitter, baffled, uncomprehending, heartbroken. Dreams of the tender daughter he drove away from home through a terrible misunderstanding . . . .

•

Resembles, superficially, an old fable about a foolish old king with two evil daughters and one good daughter. He makes a mistake about who is which and pays a terrible price. The evil girls are very evil; the good girl is very good; the old man

63

is very pathetic. Same for the Glosters, only with sons. Quite misleading . . . .

Lear's Rage

"I will do such things—what they are, yet I know not; but they shall be the terrors of the earth." He was very angry . . . .

You are angry? What don't you understand?
You are angry? What have you done wrong?

•

A demented old actor. He once played king. He once played father. The curtain has rung down, the lights are out, the theatre has emptied. But in the world beyond the proscenium arch he keeps reciting his lines and is furious that the world has forgotten its responses.

•

Rage is a sickness of the enraged.

Lear's Plan

I tried to warn him, but when he is in the grip of an idea he is as immovable as when he is in the grip of rage. Worse. He is fleetingly aware, enraged, of what he calls "the tempest in my mind" that he knows overwhelms him. But he can be lulled by calm plausibility into the disasters of reason without the sense that anything is amiss. It seems so clear, so obvious, so right. That, unfortunately, is how foolishness feels from the inside. Lear's great rage was preceded by his great folly.

He was an idealist, but oddly—or perhaps naturally—his comments on politics were usually cynical. "Get thee glass eyes, and like a scurvy politician seem to see things thou dost not." "There," speaking of a beggar running from a farmer's dog, "thou mightest behold the great image of authority—a dog's obeyed in office." "Thou rascal beadle, hold they bloody hand! Why does thou lash that whore? Strip thy own back. Thou hotly lusts to use her in that kind for which thou whip'st her." And his unforgettable: "Plate sin with gold and the strong lance of justice hurtless breaks; arm it in rags, a pygmy straw does pierce it." He knew all about the arrogance of office, big thieves and little thieves, the neglect (he blamed himself) by pomp of poverty. An idealist wounded by experience, disillusioned but not wise.

And he was not, alas, completely disillusioned. He had clung, somehow to the delusion that fairness was the cure for conflict, that if he divided his kingdom equally among claimants they would have nothing to fight about, would be satisfied with their equal shares. As if pride, ambition, jealousy were satisfied by equality. He clung also to the strange belief that the young were better, more virtuous, less selfish than the old and that if they were given the power they wanted they would exercise it more wisely, more benignly, than the old. I could not convince him that civilization depended on keeping the young out of power until they had subsided into mellowness. And, strangely, he really thought that his reward for clinging to and acting on these follies would be gratitude.

Ah, gratitude! When will we master its paradoxes? Are we gratified by a gift? Sometimes. Should we express gratitude? Of course! And are we to repay the giver? Of course not. The expectation of, the act of, repayment destroys the essence of a gift. To show one's appreciation of a genuine gift is to enjoy it to the hilt, not to warp one's life under its burden. A gift is not an investment. There is an art of giving and receiving gifts. To count on gratitude, on repayment, is to ungive a gift. Lear's daughters thanked him; they boggled at the belated price. Were they to put their lives at his disposal? It is absurd to complain of ingratitude as if it were a breach of contract. Ingratitude is an ugly thing to behold—a failure of proper thankfulness, a flaw in perception and character. But action out of gratitude has a strange quality. It does not have the austere selflessness of an act done out of duty; it does not have the beauty of an act done out of love. It has an aura of "repayment" that seems to rob an act of love or generosity of its own integrity, degrades it into something else. To complain of ingratitude is, almost, to whine without understanding, a sure sign of lack of wisdom. Poor, foolish Lear!

Loyalty

An indiscriminate, undiscerning force. A great doglike quality. Kent, Lear's dog; Oswald, Goneril's dog. Loyal to their masters. But Lear was a good master, Goneril an evil one! What is that to one's dog? Oswald served Goneril faithfully even to his death. Are we to deny his loyalty because we think her unworthy of it? Loyalty is a dog without moral judgment.

Love

Powerful, unpredictable, dangerous. The only love story in this sad affair is the story of Edmund and Goneril, with Regan, perhaps, making it a triangle. But, you protest, that wasn't love! It was lust and jealousy. How could they, those creatures, be in love with him, that adventurer? Or he with them? Love is only for good people. Of course! How stupid of me.

Wit

Wit is a plotter, schemer, warrior. Edmund had wit and, following nature, swore to win by wit what he was denied by convention. A very active mind. Matched, perhaps, by Edgar who pretended to have lost his wits but used them very shrewdly. Virtue does not sharpen wit. In the state of nature the battle of wits is settled by the sword.

Loyalty, love, wit—great natural forces, heedless of virtue, blind to good or evil. Met raw in nature they can sustain or destroy.

Edmund

A great natural force. Moral: beware of evoking natural forces for which there is no room in the house.

Cordelia

Why does Cordelia remind me of Edmund? Is it because in the families of Lear and Gloster they are the outsiders, the naturals? He by accident of birth, she by inclination and conviction? The romantic girl who despises the "hypocritical" artificiality of the established order; the illegitimate son (wherefore bastard? wherefore base?) arbitrarily discriminated against by the conventional system. One can easily imagine another story in which the alienated heiress elopes with the ambitious outsider and joins him in a war against the unjust system. She might have fallen in love with him. But she would have misunderstood him. He thirsted for what she lightly tossed aside. Her conventional sisters understood Edmund better.

•

"We are not the first," said Cordelia in defeat, "who with the best meaning have incurred the worst." Ah, "the best meaning"! The purity of her intentions was much on her mind. Please tell the King of France that I haven't done anything bad, that its just that I can't be a glib hypocrite. At the head of an invading army: it is not ambition that brings me here. Just love, and my father's rights. Others act out of gross or selfish motives. But not Cordelia. She means well. She is sincere!
Sincerity: A form of self-indulgence disguised as a virtue.
A form of aggression disguised as a virtue.
Always an excuse. But I meant well! But I was sincere!

•

A familiar family story: Cordelia crying over the letter, the news from home. The absent daughter in tears over the way the poor old parent is mistreated by the sisters who have him on their hands. Sobbing at a distance from the problem.
Suppose Cordelia had made the great sacrifice, had gone along with the game, had, in fact, told the truth—"Father, I

67

love you even more than my sisters do"—and had gotten a third of the kingdom. Would she have married Burgandy? Would Lear have stayed with them? With his hundred knights? Happily ever after? Or would he soon be asking "who am I" and hearing "My Lady's father." Would Burgandy put his foot down? Would she leave him? Happiness with Cordelia—Lear's last illusion.

●

How can we really understand Cordelia's initial action and Lear's disproportionate response? Her friends explain it as a failure of communication. Lear did not see that she really spoke out of love, that she meant only to warn him against her false sisters. But he thought, when she refused to vie with her sisters in hyperbole, that she was cold and unloving and, since he loved her most, he felt rejected and betrayed and was, therefore, enraged. But he misunderstood her, it was all a misunderstanding. He was so used to the language of the court that he had no ear for the language of the heart, the language of truth . . . .

All nonsense! The real trouble was that Lear suddenly understood her, her foolish refusal to rise to a significant social occasion, saw what it all meant, saw the deeper side of her scorn for tradition, sensed in her a crude parody of himself. He was so furious with himself that he disowned her on the spot. Who had raised her? Where was her mother, where was Mrs. Lear? Odd, now that I think of it. No Mrs. Lear. No Mrs. Gloster. None of the daughters have children. Not a mother in sight! A barren, sterile world . . . .

Retrospect

They are all dead. It is years since I stole away, a long time since I turned my back on playing the fool. But even now I cannot be sure which of the two versions that haunt me is the distortion, which the truth.

Sometimes I see Lear the magnificent, looming above the

others, majestic, brooding, a thoughtful giant among small creatures, bearing great gifts, planning great plans—torn to bits by the petty ferocity of children and subjects unable to respond to the burden of his love and idealism.

But sometimes he seems, among ordinary human beings, a shrill demented spirit, oddly stripped of common sense and ordinary perception, mad in his expectations, warped in his vision, rash, childish, destructive.

Great Lear, I think, and rehearse the story of the angel fallen to "this great stage of fools." Poor Lear, I think, and mourn his sad descent into madness. I cannot let either version go. He is good and great; they are evil dwarves. He is insane; they are normal. I start up from a nightmare of storm and fangs; it is only raining gently and the dog is whining to get in . . . .

Part Two

APOLOGIA

No? No you say, Unbalanced, perverse, wrong, all wrong. Goneril and Regan *are* monsters. Edmund is simply satanic, evil. Cordelia may be flawed, but she does come close to representing, as Auden says, "perfect love." So why are the sins of Goneril and Regan and Edmund taken so casually, minimized? Why so coldly unresponsive to Cordelia? Why so unsympathetic to Lear? Why soften the conflict between good and evil, the horror of ingratitude . . . . What it is all about is quite clear, quite terrible. Your treatment is an exercise in distortion!

My first impulse is to conceded and retreat. It sometimes does appear, even to me, unbalanced; and a defense would seem only to attempt to marshal cleverness in aid of perversity. But, upon reflection, defense, not retreat, is called for. And not merely a defense of an irresponsible privilege of interpretation. An "interpretation"—you twist a bit and squint and block out some things and exaggerate others and lo!—a caricature, a parody, a revised version, a *King Lear* somewhat warped but a possible reading. Of course it is a possible reading. But I want to say something more—that it is in fact very close to a correct reading, that it is a way of reading *Lear* that is true to its deeper theme. We are easily lulled (as was Tolstoy) into the obvious reading of an ancient fable. We see through the obvious when, altering the light, what was shadowed becomes clearer. The characters, differently illuminated, reveal their kinship to us, to the more familiar types that inhabit the common human world. The melodramatic clash between good and evil will no longer obscure the deeper theme, worthy of the work. It is, I think, a different story.

There is a puzzle about *King Lear*. It seems always to be full of significance, full of depth, of greatness. The language is magnificent. Characters emerge unforgettably. And yet it is oddly difficult to state a sustaining theme worthy of its greatness. The pathos of senility? The descent of greatness into madness? The horror of ingratitude? The awful consequences of mistakes about appearance and reality in the realm of good and evil? Something can be said for these themes, of course, but they seem, when we state them, to fall far short of the quality of the work. Can *that* be what the fuss is all about? Of course, to try to extract a "theme" always runs that risk when we are dealing with a great many-sided work. To say that it is about this or that always seems to be saying that it is less than what is richly presented to us; it is a presentation of life, not a sermon on a theme. But still, can we find a theme that, when stated, will seem suddenly to illuminate rather than diminish, to make things fall into a richer pattern than the obvious ones, to add deeper unity to what has seemed oddly diverse and even unrelated? I think so; and, if that is the case, we have an interpretation, a reading, that justifies itself. And that may justify—if indeed it does not require—a perception of the characters in an altered light. I do not mean that we are justified in an arbitrary distortion of character to fit an externally imposed theme. I mean, rather, that in the light of the theme the characters shape themselves a bit differently, although in ways not unsupported by the text.

Obviously, I think I have found such a theme. "Found" is

the right word. Once stated, it is obvious; not stated, it is easy to overlook. But it is found, not simply invented. It is, as I make explicit, the ancient contrast between nature and convention. Contrast, or conflict, or relation, or tension—between what is natural and what is conventional, artifactual, cultural, or civil. Between what is often called the "state of nature" and civil society or "culture" or "civilization"; between the world of nature and the human city; between raw nature and second nature. I do not intend here to argue the distinction or to explicate it. It is an ancient distinction, a controversial distinction, and an intriguingly important one. What is a bit novel in my reading of *King Lear* is my reading of it in the light of this distinction, as Shakespeare's "warning against unraveling the garment of ceremony and custom that stands between us and the storm of raw nature." That reading, I think, really needs no defense. It is epitomized by the two entrances of Lear: the first, the majestic king ushered in by trumpets, preceded by the symbol of the crown, attended by the court, Lear at the peak of he civic order; the second, ushered in by the storm, buffeted by raw nature, a pathetic "forked animal," soaked to the skin, stripped of the protection of the ceremonial order. What may need defense is my treatment of the characters.

Lear, of course, undergoes a shattering ordeal; and it seems to begin with a really inexplicable mistake, with an impassioned rejection of Cordelia that leaves him at the mercy of his other daughters. Even before the consequences of that act reveal themselves he appears—to Kent, to the Fool, to Goneril and Regan—to be out of his mind. How else can we account for his fatal act? Out of his mind, unbalanced, responding wildly disproportionately to Cordelia's action. By common consent, he is making a terrible mistake. But why the mistake? It does not help explain its quality to simply evoke "madness."

We need to speculate a bit about Lear before the fall. What was his state of mind? Picking up the clues that Shakespeare scatters about I portray Lear as a special sort of liberal reformer although, even as I dare say that, I shudder at the charge of parochialism that it lays me open to. He is a king; he has been king for a long time; he is not really exhausted; he has some ideas and he proposes to put them into effect. His opening speech is less an announcement of retirement or a farewell address than an inaugural address, ushering in his carefully hatched brave new world. The young are to have their places in the sun, equality is to abolish strife, there is to be no single king but, instead, a triumvirate of equal dukes—that sort of thing. I resist the temptation to play out the purely political scenario, painting the older girls as "conservatives" a bit miffed by their father's disconcerting liberalism and, even more temptingly, presenting Cordelia as a young "radical" who scorns her father's liberal reforms in favor of her deeper rejection of the hypocritical social order—leaving her father with the baffled fury of the liberal dismissed casually and unappreciated by the radical offspring. Although something of this sort is not altogether out of the picture.

I chose, instead, to stress what Lear and Cordelia have in common—a failure to appreciate the precarious conventional structure that shields us from the raw forces of the state of nature. Between them they strike the dolorous blow that cracks the civic armour and lets raw nature in—the nature that storms, ravages, torments, horrifies us with a glimpse of what lies all around us, beneath mere manners. So I see Lear as a good-hearted, naive, optimistic social reformer, full of hope for the plans he reveals at the opening of the play, driven to fury by the unexpected rejection by Cordelia, not quite understanding it, but sensing, nevertheless, that it is more than harmless petulance. And the world begins to fall apart. That is, Lear begins his journey from the height of civility to the depths of nature.

I am haunted by the image of Lear as the old magician maintaining, through his art, a precarious balance among partly tamed, partly slumbering monsters; maintaining a control that might, if he is not careful, slip away, leaving him at the mercy of the forces yawning and stretching into their awakening. A trial run at Prospero with Caliban slipping out of control. I see him presiding over the court over which he has cast a civilizing spell—a spell broken by the rebellion of Cordelia and by Lear's shocked impotence in the face of his favorite's rejection of ritual, of the magic formula, of artificial manners and phrases, of all that insincere hocus-pocus—the hocus-pocus that has, in fact, kept the beasts subdued, that now begins to lose its power.

For the full horror of Lear's ordeal to be grasped we must see it not simply as the consequence of an act of rage, of infirmity, of senility. The ordeal is peculiarly the ordeal of the idealist, the well-intentioned reformer, the good-natured master of revels who has forgotten what the world is like with its masks off. He must bring it on himself; he must be inexcusably ignorant. Like, in short, King Lear. And indeed, considering what a king must do, what a king must know, what a king is for—it is not so clear that Lear is, as he will pathetically claim, "more sinned against than sinning." But it is impossible, in the end, not to pity him. All this, at least, I have already said through the soliloquies of Goneril and Edmund and made more explicit in the Fool's Notebook.

What needs more defense, I suppose, is my treatment of the sisters. I do not treat them, I do not accept the treatment of them, as if they are another trio like Cinderella and her two mean sisters. Nor do I intend a perverse reversal of the situation. I do not think Cordelia is as good as she is usually taken to be; I do not think the other two may be as bad as they can seem—although they are bad enough. But that is not really the point. What they are and what they represent can best be grasped when they are seen in relation to the nature-convention theme.

The older sisters are presented to us initially as conventional duchesses, well behaved, restrained by the conventional ceremony of political and daughterly propriety. When the traditional ceremonial order is disrupted by Lear's program and rage, they become increasingly unmannerly, increasingly shameless in the indulgence of the passions once held under constraint by Lear functioning as father and king. They reveal their deeper natures, unleashed. Conventionally shaped ambition gets out of hand, burgeoning insatiably, increasingly cruel in its manifestations, shamelessly erotic, unfaithful, ungrateful. We learn what they (we?) are really like beneath

73

the mask of civility. As Lear opens the floodgates to the forces of nature they fall increasingly under the sway of the law of the state of nature, the state of war, of force and fraud.

I do not quite want to assert that Goneril and Regan are simply normal human beings acting as any person might act when the conventional order is supplanted by the natural order. (New York when the power fails?) But I do not think, either, that we should be allowed to dismiss them as simply "evil" without considering how akin they may be to relatively normal human animals freed from the restraints of civility. Do we really need to be reminded today of the forms that self-centered impatience toward parents may take, of the varieties of filial cruelty we are adept at?

As for Cordelia! You either recognize the rebellious, idealistic youth or you do not. If you do, I need not labor the point. If you do not, I am afraid I would labor it in vain. She is a romantic rebel against the artifices of society. Her feelings are mixed—far from unadulterated love. You have only to notice her bitterness to her sisters to realize that. She is mixed, and complicated but, essentially, she is young, undisciplined, full of theories, and uncompromising. I will not say more about her, for to do so would be to seem to criticize a young woman for being a particular sort of young woman who, with luck, will outgrow it all. It would be churlish to attack the child. It is foolish to become maudlin over her. She did not understand what she was doing.

My treatment of the sisters seems strange only if we begin with an oversimplified insistence that one is good and the other two evil. Or if we think that the real story is the story as it appears to the distraught, tormented mind of Lear. Why do we think we see truly when we see the world through Lear's eyes? Do we think he saw Cordelia clearly? Of course not. Do we think he saw Goneril clearly when she objected to his hundred knights? Probably we do, although it is interesting that Shakespeare does not tell us who is right in the quarrel. Why do we assume that her complaint is groundless, unreasonable, viciously selfish? It is a deeper play if we broaden the range of our sympathy a bit and try to see more than Lear saw. That is why I risk having Goneril tell what I think of as "Goneril's Love Story"—which, by the way, is true to the text. And why I let Edmund impose his view of things on us, and risk a long shot by comparing him with Jacob. The lines of *King Lear* do not need to be rewritten; they should be read more carefully.

But the tendency to confuse a character with an over-simplified reading of it is a difficult one to cure. Consider the way we treat Kent and Oswald. I cannot remember a production in which Oswald is not presented—gratuitously and with little support from the text—in a strongly unfavorable light, as an out and out villain. Probably because he is the faithful servant of the evil Goneril. But I suggest that there is a deeper point presented for our consideration—that loyalty has an indiscriminate quality, that it is possible to be loyal in a bad cause, that loyalty may not be enough. Oswald is as devotedly loyal to his cause as Kent is to his. His last thought, as he is dying, is for the carrying out of his mission—loyal to the very end. Sometime I would like to see Kent and Oswald played by twins, both presented sympathetically, so that we might have to think about the chance or fate that summons our loyalty to this or that cause, that directs our faithful service to Caesar or to Brutus, to Troy or to Greece. Kent and Oswald have much in common. They show us contrasting modes of loyal service—the critical and the uncritical. Kent criticizes Lear to his face, out of loyalty; Oswald is uncritically loyal in his service. A decent reading gives us, as a bonus, the problem of freedom of speech and loyalty. But no, it is easier to read Oswald as an evil servant of evil. I invite you to peruse the text for evidence.

And now about Edmund. I do not want to repeat what I have said about Edmund in allowing him to speak for himself. But what the Gloster story adds to the Lear story, beyond repetition of the theme of filial ingratitude and failure to distinguish between good and bad children is the explicit legitimate-natural dichotomy. The great fact about Edmund is that he is illegitimate, without real status in the established order. If there is to be a place for him he must get it by breaking in. He is nature erupting into the city. It misses the point to add him simply to the evil team. So I am at some pains to present him in something of a sympathetic light, as the outsider who, through no fault of his own, finds himself outside the charmed world, as if he were a member of some tolerated minority—tolerated but firmly excluded from the inner circle. Edmund is, of course, unscrupulous; but that is something that, today, would not lack apologists. After all, it would be said, the social discrimination between Edmund and Edgar is unjust, unearned, unmerited. Why should Edmund stand for it, accept it meekly as his lot? Why should he be scrupulous against injustice. Scruples are luxuries, ornaments for insiders. After we have established a just order, then we can ask that everyone act scrupulously .... Edmund's "Thou, Nature, art my Goddess" is miles from Satan's "Evil be thous my good," but I am not going to press a point that seems so obvious to me. Disparity for disparity, Jacob is a better starting point than Satan. It is worth trying to read Edmund sympathetically if we can; and if we can, the play becomes a deeper tragedy. And Shakespeare always intends the deeper tragedy.

So this is my defense against the charge of giving a perverse reading of *King Lear*: I have stated, properly, the deep theme of the play; and I have read the characters, consistently with the text, in a way that is consonant with the theme. And the theme and the characters, thus read, enrich and support each other.

The Limping King

He is one of those to whom the world presents itself as something to be solved. It does not lie before him as a rich gift to be enjoyed, a home mysteriously prepared for his occupancy, a landscape simply content to be itself. What does it mean? He peers at it, brooding, worried, searching for signs. Everything means something else, carries a message, must be deciphered, unriddled. He cannot fall asleep until the day has been solved. Quick, suspicious, mind leaping, agile, impatient. If he were to walk slowly he might not limp. But he is always hurrying, hurrying as if late, limping, resenting the delay, urgent, headlong, pressing. What is it? What is it? What's the problem?

When Creon arrived with the message from Delphi, Oedipus lost no time. He would save the city again. He would cure it, rid it of its pollution. He would unravel the oddly neglected mystery of the death of the old king and punish the criminal. To work! Track down old rumors, summon witnesses, send for old Tiresias. I'll get to the bottom of this, he assures the plagued city. You know me; I'm good at this sort of thing!

What was it like on the eve of disaster? The visitor to Thebes would have toured the seven gates of the great walled city. Splendid, but oddly hollow and disquieting, inhabitants preoccupied and subdued. No teeming throngs of careless children; adult faces etched with anxiety and disappointment. Murmurs, if one could overhear them, of failure, sickness, death. A pervasive air of depression, the sense that life was sterile, fruitless, empty. Something was wrong, something so generally wrong as to seem beyond specific treatment, hopeless.

So, a troubled city, a diligent king eager to deal with the trouble, willing to consult the experts. And the oracular message, when it comes, brings hope. There is something that needs to be done, that can be done. There is another puzzle to be solved by the quick-witted king.

AT DELPHI

Sir, a delegation from Thebes.

What's the problem?

The usual—crop failure, infant mortality, epidemics—they seem to be having a bad time.

I see. Well, tell them they have a sick society, rotten, polluted, corrupt. Tell them to get rid of their pollution.

Of course, sir, I told them that. But the spokesman is quite persistent; he wants to know what pollution in particular.

Oh? Well, just tell them it's because of their government, their ruler, whoever he is. Bound to be corrupt; probably got rid of his predecessor. That's it. Tell them to punish the killer of the last king. That should stir them into healthy activity. Anything else? Right, but make a note about Thebes . . . no, wait. Don't you still have a case study to do? Well, do it on this one. Follow it up, get the background, the whole story, including the deep implications. But please, I've had enough of "Ambiguity and Inevitability in Oracular Discourse." Keep it simple, skip the jargon, and above all try to remember that you're dealing with human beings. They just haven't had your advantages.

Yes, sir.

•

Another riddle to solve and the city would be saved again.
Yes, again. Oedipus had done it once before. He had rescued
the city from the Sphinx, had answered the question by which
the city had been terrorized. It is not an episode easy to
understand. There is the riddle of the Sphinx; and there is the
puzzle about the riddle.

The riddle itself seems simple. It is about feet. What is it that
goes on four in the morning, two at noon, and three in the
evening? Ask a lifelong limper a riddle about feet and the
chances are he has heard that one before. "Man," answers
Oedipus in a flash, ask me a hard one! But the Sphinx vanishes
in baffled rage, and Oedipus the liberator hobbles on to glory.
Man, of course. First he crawls, then he walks upright, then
he totters on a cane—infant, adult, codger. Man is the strange
beast, enduring through stages.

Shall we leave it as a fairy tale? A monster preys on a city,
seizes a passer-by, poses a question, crushes the tongue-tied
victim, spreading terror—until a stranger gives the right
answer, frees the city and is made king by the grateful people.
Another story of a local tyrant slain by a bright young wanderer
who then marries the heiress or the princess or the childless
widow-queen and settles down to rule happily ever after? Is
the particular riddle only incidental—any would do—or does
it have a special appropriateness? Thebes, I think, was oppressed
by its failure to understand something fundamental and
obvious. It did not understand something about infancy,
maturity, old age. It did not understand generation,
regeneration through generational succession, the proper
relation of generations. It was a city in which—if we may draw
an inference from the botched royal infanticide with which the
story begins—a child can be seen as a threat to the parent, a
city in which a parent is, perversely, a danger to the infant,
a city in which, as for poor Oedipus, home is not a place of

79

refuge. A world turned inside out, a place of generational terror. The riddle was a riddle for that sort of place.

Oedipus, we are told, had come to power through his victory over the Sphinx. He not only gave the right answer to an interesting question; he confounded and banished a dreaded questioner; he rescued Thebes from questioning. He took over; he had all the answers. But it may be a mistake to think that somehow he set Thebes straight. More likely, it was the same old Thebes, uncured, unquestioning, drifting, therefore, without understanding into deeper and more painful fruitlessness—crops fail, children die—and once again Oedipus sets out to deal with a problem by trying to solve a riddle.

What is plaguing Thebes? The answer from Delphi is that Thebes neglects justice. A king has been killed and the city has not bothered to find and punish the killer. It cannot be indifferent to justice and expect to thrive. Who killed King Laius? Who spoiled Thebes? Who, moving unexposed among us is the secret sinner whose action has poisoned the wells of legitimacy, whose unpunished act leaves justice wounded? Find out! Expose! Correct!

Oedipus, full of virtuous zeal, is inclined to lecture. Each of you, he says to the suffering citizens, feels his own private pain; but I, the king, must bear the pain of each of you, the city's pain. You care about your private interests; I must care for the public interest. But, Oedipus adds, as if such a strange idea carries little conviction, I have a heavy private stake in this as well. If there are assassins around I am the most likely target. And I have a personal connection with Laius, since I married his widow. He proclaims that his edict against the murderer applies to everyone, to the king himself as well as to any other person. No one is to be above the law.

With this fanfare the great investigation is launched. Oedipus summons Tiresias. But he and the canny old seer do not get along very well. Tiresias refuses to have anything to do with the investigation, although it is clear that he knows something. Oedipus is outraged. How can you refuse to help the city? How can you refuse to answer? Can it be—his mind leaping to the obvious conclusion—that the answer would incriminate you, that you were a party to a conspiracy?

Tiresias, enraged by the accusation, turns on Oedipus. You want me to talk, do you? You really want to know who did it? All right. You did! You killed King Laius! And there is something wrong with your family life too! You want my answer? There it is!

How must this appear to Oedipus, standing at the height of his powers, an honored liberator-king, diligent in his concern for his subjects, devoted to his wife and children, facing a knotty civic crisis? Far behind him, not altogether forgotten, lies his troubled childhood and youth in Corinth, the passions and confusions from which he had fled in baffled dismay (but that was in a different city . . .). Nearer lie the memories of his life in the new world, the struggles along the dusty road, living by one's wits, some bits of luck, success, esteem, the rise to power, to where he now stands, bruises not showing, father to all his simple subjects. Of course he does not accept the absurd accusation.

It is a familiar situation, is it not? How often have we enjoyed the spectacle of the pillar of society accused of some crime by a strange witness—an outsider, a nobody, a shady character, a quack in the grip of an insight. Who, after all, is Tiresias that we should believe him? A lone crank moving mysteriously on the edge of things, an aged creature with a strange history. He is blind, but he seems to hear everything, collects and stores away odd bits of information. "A little bird told me," he once said, and the peasants now believe he talks with birds. But he really gets it all from the servants. His special knowledge is the downstairs whisper—who slept with whom, what happened to the baby, who sold the bracelet . . . . He specializes in the inside story, the report from the valet, the delivery man, the faithful servant to whom a package is entrusted. They bring morsels to him at the center of his weird web. Omniscient, feared, a bad creature to cross. We hate to have to believe him. But unfortunately, incredibly, his information is accurate and will soon be seen by all the world to be so. "You are the killer you seek!" And with these words Oedipus is transformed from royal investigator into frantic defendant.

I suppose it is possible to think that Oedipus knew he had killed the king, that he thought he had gotten away with it, that faced with belated exposure he thought he could brazen it out raising the plausible cry of conspiracy. But I don't think that is the case. He does not know he is guilty.

There is a difference between doing something and knowing, realizing, what it is that you have done. Oedipus could be brought to remember that, some time ago, he had killed some people, including an irascible old man, in a furious traffic brawl. It may not have troubled his dreams, but mention of the place where the three roads meet brought it all back. But . . . but . . . was that old King Laius? Didn't the old report say the king was killed by a band of men? If so, then the man killed by Oedipus was someone else. Send for the surviving witness! Oedipus clings to hope, praying for coincidence. There is a coincidence, but it will not be one he will welcome.

So Oedipus knew he had killed an old man; he did not know he had killed the king. Knowledge lies concealed in layers. We glimpse a surface and we act. We do not know, we learn with difficulty, the complicated plots in which we play a part, the layers of identities beneath the faces. Furious old man; beneath that, king; beneath that . . . . We do not know who they are when we brush them aside; we do not know all that we are either.

In the attempt to solve the puzzle of the king's death another story is going to reveal itself. We will learn that Oedipus has killed one of his fathers. Yes, one of his fathers, a sort of father, a poor sort of father, an anti-father in effect. Polybus, the one who adopted him and raised him as his son was another father. What is the correct description? Laius, real father; Polybus, apparent father? Or, Laius, mere fatherer; Polybus significant father? Are we concerned with biology or with real life? At any rate, Oedipus, running away from home, from his fostering father and mother, kills the man who was his mere biological father and marries the woman who was his mere biological mother. "Mere" understates the case, or overstates it. They had intended infanticide and thought they had succeeded. But stated crudely, it is discovered that Oedipus had killed his father and married his mother.

There are moments when it seems we might be spared the anguish of enlightenment. Tiresias at first wants no part in the investigation. Jocasta, at a crucial point, urges her husband-son to leave it alone. But he persists. His urge to know, to get to the bottom of the story, to settle all doubts, to be satisfied with nothing but the whole truth—admirable, is it not?—is overpowering. Oedipus is the model of the uncompromising investigator, the undeterrable truth-seeker.

Against all this, the despairing wisdom of Jocasta. Stop it, leave it alone, she says. Life is a matter of chance. Don't stir up the ashes of the past. Don't try to outwit the future. Take things as they come, without superstitious fears and omens, without pointless curiosity. Enjoy the present. Stop this restless prying! She has learned from bitter experience. Long ago her first husband credulous about oracles destroyed their new-born infant. Stupid fears of the future. Was Laius to have been immortal, or to die when and how he wished? Men are children, excited by words, moved by abstractions. There are Oedipus and Creon raging in public, in an unseemly political quarrel. Creon, go home! Oedipus, come into the house! Now, Oedipus, what was that all about? You two should make up . . . . Motherly Jocasta in a world of children and charlatans. Clever restless Oedipus, worrying, worrying, always wanting answers. For heavens sake, stop it! (What, we wonder, did Jocasta know, and when did she know it?)

We are poised for a moment on the brink of revelation, torn between the lust to unmask, expose, to see the world in its naked disarray, to revel in the destructive revolt against appearances and surfaces, to wallow to the bottom of things, to find the discreditable and discrediting truth, to dispel illusion, to come at last, as Yeats says, "into the desolation of reality"; and, on the other hand, battered a bit by the world and grateful for small favors, the desire to leave some life-sustaining illusions undisturbed, to enjoy the consolations of appearances, greenness and the dancing patterns of light and shade on a mere surface, the sometimes splendid facade, the world enjoyed without iconoclasm, a world familiar although not understood. Behold Oedipus the king, Oedipus the loving husband, loving father of four. Behold the Theban Royal Family! The Theban Royal Family? Let us do some research. Who are they, really. Not what they seem. Look closely. The splendor will fade . . . .

Poised for a moment, ready to sink back into warm ignorance, but Oedipus cannot be stopped and finally gets to the terrible facts. The scandal is revealed. Jocasta kills herself—too much wife, too much mother. Oedipus blinds himself—those unperceiving eyes—and gropes toward his long exile.

A LESSON FOR AGNOSTICS

Respect the gods! Laius was warned by the gods not to have a son by Jocasta, for if he did, the son would kill him. But impious Laius fathered a son and, thinking to escape the divine decree, ordered the infant put to death. But the boy was saved by a servant and adopted by the childless royal couple of another city. When the lad, Oedipus, grew up, he was warned by an oracle that he would kill his father and marry his mother. To avoid this fate he fled from what he thought was his home. But he ran to meet his destiny. For he ran to his real home, killed his father and married his mother, not knowing who they were. But eventually the truth—prophecies fulfilled—was revealed, the power of the gods demonstrated, religion vindicated. So much for scoffers!

THE HERO AS HAPLESS VICTIM

An unlucky man, this is his story. What happens to us is quite independent of our merits. We are born into situations we do not choose, and some seem made for misfortune. Like poor Oedipus. Parents who rejected him, maimed him, put him out to die. Not his fault! He survived by luck, was adopted and raised with love. When he grew up he left home for what he thought were the best of reasons. How could he know that the imperious old man who attacked him on the road, whom he killed in self-defense, was his father and the King of Thebes to boot. No one told him. And then, using his intelligence, he saved Thebes. Hailed as savior he was made king, married the attractive widow-queen, settled down to rule, raised a nice family. And then, years later, his investigation of an old crime—a clear duty of his office—and the revelation of what he had unknowingly done—that he had killed his father and married his mother. Was it really his fault? How could he have known? It was not fair, not just! He was not guilty. He was just unlucky!

REPORT BY CANDIDATE—PRIEST AT DELPHI

Why do they come to us? As long as people must live and act in a world of which they are largely ignorant they will, unless their ignorance is really too great, their pride too swollen, seek advice. What to do? How to know what to do? Come to the great consultant, come to Delphi. Alas, they seek information; they need wisdom.

We have developed advising into a high art. Yes, it is an art and a difficult one. It is not just knowing what to say. How to say it . . . but I am not to do a disquisition on Delphic theory and practice. I am to do an analysis of the case of the unfortunate Oedipus as it is influenced by oracles. But I may, I hope, be permitted a few general remarks. If you give advice to someone who is ignorant or clever—I'm not sure which is worse—he is probably going to misunderstand it. Also, if someone strikes you as needing advice you can be sure that what makes him need advice will probably keep him from following it. Finally—yes, I'll get to Oedipus—we give advice, but that does not mean that we have some special way of looking into the future, that we know what is going to happen, as if it had already happened. A good adviser understands a great deal, but the belief that he has some sort of crystal ball is sheer superstition . . . yes, Oedipus . . . .

The First Oracle—The Unwelcome Child

There seems to have been a prediction that if King Laius had a son the son would kill him. I say "seems" because it has been very difficult to track the story down, and it is impossible at this distance to disentangle general fears and warnings from specific predictions. It is clear, however, that the child was not merely unwanted; he was feared. Many children are, of course, unexpected, unhoped for, and in some sense unwanted. But it is odd to think of an infant as actually feared. Helpless, tiny, crying to be saved from nothingness by parental love. Feared? Yet that is the first hard fact about Oedipus; the new-born infant was feared by his father, King Laius. Evidently, when Laius looked at the infant what he saw, grimly, was his own destruction at the hands of this as yet vulnerable, as yet infantile destroyer. Believing that he saw what the future held for him he did not wait until it was too late, until the danger was clear and present. He prudently struck first, to destroy the destroyer while he was still vulnerable. In self-defense he ordered infanticide.

Prediction? Oracle? There is a story that because of something Laius did the gods decreed that if he were to have a son by Jocasta the son would kill him. Such stories about the gods are always springing up, and we are taught here to deal with them without scandalizing the devout. That is, we are taught to interpret them gently and instructively. In the fundamentalist version poor Oedipus is the divinely appointed executioner of the god-offending Laius, the unlucky chosen instrument against whom Laius must struggle in vain.

Laius, one gathers, was something of a terror. It is hard to find anything nice to say about him. A very model of those who think they see the future clearly and are willing to act ruthlessly to forestall the evil they see. Sometimes they are idealistic, but in his case merely hard, selfish, cunning, quick-tempered, cruel and, I am afraid, stupid. We would classify him, among our clients, with those upon whom good advice is utterly wasted. What led specifically to the bungled attempt at infanticide must be a matter of speculation, but given Laius' character it would not have taken much: "Enjoy yourself while you can, King Laius, because if it is a boy you won't be king in this house anymore!"; or "Laius I warn you! You will make his life miserable. Sooner or later he'll kill you, if you don't kill him first!"; or "Who will take my crown from me? My son? We'll see about that!" Some conception or misconception turned the hapless infant into a terrible menace. I do not doubt that Laius was acting in what he thought was self-defense when he ordered the infant destroyed. He thought that a menace should be nipped in the bud.

Of course, the job was bungled. Or rather, the would-be killer, acting coldly on his vision of the future, was frustrated by a simple servant acting out of sheer animal warmth. Planners and peasants! So, instead of killing his son as he supposes, Laius merely succeeds in laming him. And there is a persistent irony about the laming. Why it was necessary to pin the feet of the infant I do not know, but the rescued victim had trouble with his feet all his life. He even got his name, poor babe, from his swollen feet, and he hobbled and limped. He was never able to run as well as other lads and came to shun running games. Sought the shade and became very good at puzzles—slow-footed, quick-witted, a young intellectual. Much later, running away from his childhood home, limping towards Thebes and a new life, he does not move out of the way of a chariot fast enough. Impatient old Laius, furious at the delay takes a swing at him, at his unrecognized son (something oddly annoying about the fellow). The weary hobbler, assaulted, flies into a rage (ah, heredity!) and kills the old man. The battered child's revenge—a life for a sore foot. And Oedipus plods on to encounter the Sphinx and read the limpid riddle . . . .

The so-called first oracle. It is evoked to explain how Laius was driven to reject his son, how, in hope of escaping a dreaded destiny, acting in self-defense, he ordered that his son be put to death. Lower-class sentimentality kept the infant alive, however, rejected, battered, and in need of foster care . . . .

The Second Oracle or Running Away From Home

I come now to the second oracle—it's possible influence on

the flight from Corinth. Why did Oedipus run away from home? Why did the unwanted one flee from where he was loved and wanted? What part did we play in the crisis?

It was not an unhappy home. Polybus and Merope raised him as their own son, never told him he had been adopted, even denied it indignantly when malicious gossip reached his ears. He grew up an heir apparent, loved, overindulged perhaps, a bit too clever, no real friends his own age, easily upset, socially awkward, home loving. And yet, one day in young manhood he fled from his home in a panic. The popular story is that Oedipus, upset by persistent innuendo that he was not the child of Polybus and Merope, stole off to ask us who his parents were. But we, the story goes (and this is even Oedipus' wrapped version), met him with "Begone, wretch! You are going to kill your father and marry your mother!" Staggered, Oedipus, forgetting his original question, turned his back on Corinth and fled toward Thebes. (Travel, he will discover, is no cure for an identity crisis.) And why did we treat him this way? To get him to Thebes so that he would fulfill the first oracle! Well,he did return to Thebes, not knowing it was a return. He did kill King Laius. He did marry his mother. But the notion that he had to return to Thebes so that he would be able to do these things is an example of a popular fallacy for which there should be a name.

It is true that we did not answer the question he came to ask, but there is a simple explanation. "Who are my real parents? Is my mother's husband really my father? Who am I, really? . . ." It is our policy not to answer that sort of question (of course, we have many ways of not answering a question). We are not a family certification bureau. We do, naturally, since requests for advice are often introduced by confessions, have a good deal of information about these matters. But we have a commitment to confidentiality. Our position depends on it. We don't peddle secrets; we don't betray confidences. It is an institutional necessity—something not shared or felt by a lone wolf like Tiresias who collects gossip from his servile informers (no sane person would confess anything to him) and uses the information irresponsibly and even vindictively. So of course we did not answer the question Oedipus sneaked away from home to ask us.

The other thing, the warning, the prediction, the "doom," is a more complicated matter. I have managed (diligence and a bit of luck!) to find the priest who was on duty that day. The episode seems to have made an impression on him. Garrulous but very clear headed, great memory, and eager to tell me more than I wanted to know. The gist of his story, severely edited, goes: "A young man, very upset. Nervous, introverted, impulsive. Hobbled badly. Well dressed. Pampered. Mama's boy. All this obvious at a glance. 'Is Polybus really my father,' he blurted out. Barely civil. I wasn't going to answer that, of course, but I thought it rather enterprising for a youngster. If a father comes storming in and asks if his son is really his son I give him short shrift. A husband who asks is a fool; a son who asks is a victim, worth a bit of attention. 'Did they adopt me?' he pressed. That changed the picture. Not one parent but both in question. 'And do you ever dream?', I asked, teasing, hoping to calm him, 'that you would get rid of him and live happily ever after with her?' I was startled by his reaction. He turned white and stared open-mouthed for a long moment, turned abruptly and hobbled out. That was the last time I tried humor with disturbed young men. I knew it was a mistake. I even tried to follow him, but he scudded away as if pursued by demons. Never saw him again. I was severely reprimanded by my supervisor. Don't think I'll ever forget that episode . . ."

Oedipus obviously did not forget that episode either, although it is inaccurate to say that he remembered it—remembered it correctly, that is. The night-sobbed fantasy of getting rid of him and living happily ever after with her is, as we all know, common enough. But Oedipus did not know that, (Jocasta tried in vain to explain it to him later) thought he was unique, thought the priest had seen through him to his special wickedness. Ah, well. The innocent flee when no man pursueth. He ran away hardly able, hardly wanting to distinguish between desire, fantasy, warning, prediction. It remained with him as a half-buried sense of doom. He had gone to Delphi and the priest had told him that he was destined to kill his father and marry his mother and raise a repulsive brood—that is how he told the story years later. I suppose we are partly to blame. We held up a comic mirror and let him frighten himself. So much for the second oracle.

The Third Oracle

This one is quite different. The first oracle had to do with a parental attempt to deal with an unwelcome child, with infanticide parading as an act of self-defense. We were not responsible for whatever may have gone on in Laius' brutal mind. The second oracle centers on leaving home, running away from home, by a youngster disturbed by an awareness of lingering infantile patricidal and incestuous urges during a severe identity crisis. We did not urge him to run away from home, although a friend, if he had had one, might well advised him to break away and try life in a different city. He did leave home and, in fact, had a rather spectacular career. A real success story—king, husband, father. A bit vain about his mind, but he owed a great deal to his wits. He had survived the perils of infancy and adolescence and was living a decent life, doing a good job, when we, unnecessarily I believe, brought him down in ruins. By the third oracle.

There is no doubt about our role in the debacle. We sent Creon back to Thebes with the word that Thebes would continue to suffer until it found and punished the killer of King Laius. Oedipus launched the investigation and ended up with the whole story. This time he did not escape exposure. You will note that I have called a debacle what some of my colleagues regard as a great triumph. A very senior priest says that he cannot remember another case about which opinion in the college is so bitterly divided. Fortunately, outsiders are not aware of our internal disputes; we protect the innocent faith in our infallibility. But we, ourselves, do not enjoy the luxury of simple faith. The adviser who really thinks he is beyond error is a menace. Priesthood is a burden, not a pleasure, and . . . but I must curb this tendency to parade the obvious.

Some of us profess not to see what all the fuss is all about. Our oracle, they say, led to the discovery of the truth. Oedipus did kill his father; he did marry his mother. So now everyone, including Oedipus, has some additional information about the world. We did not make that world; we try to understand it, to learn the truth about it, to help others discover the truth about it if they come to us for help. Don't kill your father! Don't marry your mother! And don't expect us to cover it all up if you do. We decline, they say, to feel remorse for spreading the truth. Whatever the consequences.

I do not find this "purist" faction quite to my taste, but I respect it. I find it hard to respect the "opportunists" among us. They seem pleased and rather smug. "Look," I heard one of them say, "I admit there was no grand design. We did not plan The Rejection, The Return, The Execution, The Marriage, The Revelation as a unified plot. But the public certainly has had its imagination caught. Too wild, people say, to be just coincidence. It must be the gods! This is the best thing that's happened to religion in a long time. People are now flocking to the shrines. If religion is better than irreligion—and I think we agree that it is—we should welcome whatever strengthens it. Prophecy is in again and we are riding high and for us to be respected is good for the whole Greek world. Oedipus' misfortune, the world's gain. We should exploit it. A chance like this comes along only once in a generation." This faction does not advocate actually cultivating superstition, but it is willing to make use of it in a good cause.

The serious question has to do with the salvation of Thebes and what we call the "second exposure" of Oedipus. We were consulted about the welfare of Thebes. We oracled. Did we give them good advice? Or were we, as some of us think, gratuitously mischievous? What was wrong with Thebes? What advice did it need? It is agreed that Thebes was a sick city. It suffered from fruitlessness. Blighted, a general failure of nurturing, self-centered and, therefore, dying. Not an untypical modern city, a dangerous place for children. And, at the time of the third oracle going through a spell of external disaster that intensified the general malaise. A sick city having a run of hard luck.

Some of us tend to blame it all on the political system. Every social ill, it is said, is a form of injustice, and the cure is justice. Respect for law is basic, and who will respect the law if regicide is not punished? You may not be able to set a society straight all at once, but insisting on justice, on the punishment of regicide, is as good a place as any to begin. And if it can be shown that no one, not even a king, is above the law, so much the better. On this view, telling Thebes to find and punish the killer of Laius was exactly the right thing to do. Oedipus should not have been allowed to profit by his crime even if he made a pretty good job of being king. He did not have clean hands. He was a killer.

"Even if he made a pretty fair job of being king!" A rather grudging concession. As if intelligent rulers come along every day. "Clean hands!" Show me some one in public life with clean hands and I'll show you a failure, a holier-than-thou nonentity. So Oedipus was a politician! Coming to power is a messy business. Justice is a quality of its proper exercise, not of its acquisition. Every regime begins with the death of the old king, no matter how he may die. Become a just society! If that was the point of our advice to Thebes it was oracular in the worst sense of the word. What should we do about our sickness? Get well! Our pollution? Clean it up! Of course, of course. But suggesting that the way to do that was by launching an investigation into some forgotten old crime, by digging up some dirt about the past—typical of these irresponsible truth-mongers. There is a time to tell the truth and a time to be silent. Judgement is required, not a dogmatic appeal to a plausible principle. So part, a fragment of the truth about the death of Laius was revealed. Are we really to suppose that Oedipus was the cause of the Theban woe, that sending him into exile was the cure? That politics would become more enlightened, government more just? Too naive, even for young priests. No, the revelation was simply a delicious scandal, a boon to gossip, a tonic for every scoffer lurking on the fringes of any attempt to be decent in a rough world, eager to disabuse the trusting about the establishment. The cynics had a field day; the simple minded took refuge in superstition; and the cause of rational government, represented by King Oedipus, suffered a set-back. Our contribution to the welfare of Thebes?

Our differences over the political aspects of the case are quite bitter, but there is a group that considers politics entirely beside the point. When a society is sick, they say, politics is neither the cause nor the cure. Law, justice—mere baubles! Everything is rooted in the family—the breeding ground, the womb, the fundamental unit of humanity. There is a proper familial order and when it is distorted, scorned, warped, nothing can prosper. Father, mother, child—that is what matters, not king, subject, law. A society is sick when its families are out of order. If you can accept infanticide don't bore us with your hollow drivel about justice. What are the elemental familial disorders? Infanticide, parricide, fratricide, incest. Interesting, is it not, that Oedipus was involved in most of them. The Olympians, unfortunately, are not very helpful. Zeus is supposed to have escaped infanticide at his father's hands, to have subsequently overthrown his father, to have married his own sister . . . . It is a bit difficult to denounce Zeus. Fortunately, we could make a horrible example of Oedipus. We didn't make him do these things, but at least we contributed to his exposure. Regicide was almost the least of his sins . . . .

(The rest of the candidate-priest's report seems to be missing.)

COMMENT BY SENIOR PRIEST ON CANDIDATE'S REPORT

On the whole, an acceptable piece of work. The candidate is intelligent and imaginative. Sometimes I miss the good old days when we would, once in a while, get a bright young candidate who was—how should I put it—a bit religious. But this is the young man we all remember for the remark that our motto, "Know Thyself," means "Figure it out for yourself—don't ask us!" In the ashes of piety, wit is a consolation.

I agreed, as you will remember, to look at the candidate's

work and report to the Senior Council on what it reveals about the quality of the training we are giving to those who will inherit from us the responsibility for maintaining the high standards for which Delphi is famous. If this candidate is typical we need not be too pessimistic, although, of course, there are some problems . . . .

It *is* a problem, or eventually can become one, that nowhere in the report is there the slightest acceptance of the reality of the divine or the supernatural. We have taught him, the candidate says, to "interpret" what he thinks of as manifestations of popular superstition so as to find a perfectly natural explanation that will make sense, while allowing the vulgar to continue to live by their childish fables. Each of the oracles is stripped, in his account, of every shred of mystery. Why does Laius try to kill his infant son? Fear. Why the fear? An analysis of Laius' character is sketched, quite inconclusively, to explain the attempted infanticide. Not for a moment is it considered that a revelation was involved. No, what might have happened that might have been taken or mistaken by the ignorant as a divine revelation about the intertwined fates of father and son—that is the line taken by our bright young man. And the second oracle! I don't know whether to laugh or cry over the feeble research venture that dredged up a garrulous old-timer with a clear memory (now *that* is a miracle) of a feeble jest that sent poor Oedipus fleeing in despair. Shows what nonsense our enlightened youth will swallow rather than even consider that we could have seen Oedipus' destiny written on his face or in the stars or in "some sort of crystal ball," or in the "babbling" of an inspired woman. I'm sure we can't survive without recruiting talent; but talent without faith is something we will need, in the long run, to worry about.

Nor does our candidate take the idea of a fixed fate, an unavoidable destiny, very seriously. He declines, in short, to treat what will happen as if it had already happened, so that trying to avoid one's fate is like trying to prevent what has already happened. Sound enough. Many strange things have happened and will happen, and some of the things we try to avoid will happen anyway and sometimes, most intriguingly, what we want to avoid will happen precisely because of what we do to prevent its happening. As in the case of Oedipus. To avoid killing his father and marrying his mother he ran away from home. If he had not done that, he would not have done what he tried to avoid. I suspect that the self-defeating futility of his attempt to avoid what he wanted to avoid is a more interesting feature of the story than what it was that he tried, and failed, to avoid. I have heard it whispered that poor Oedipus really *wanted* to kill his father and marry his mother— that he killed Laius because he reminded him of Polybus and that he married Jocasta because she reminded him of Merope. About as silly as the "unavoidable destiny" version.

I am surprised to find him coming down, in the case of the third oracle, on the side of not exposing the truth about Oedipus. More mature than I had expected, and I gather from his remarks that this is a controversial point about which we have no clear policy. I confess that as I grow older I find myself less inclined to think that problems can be solved by simply finding and proclaiming the truth, more protective of the persisting illusions (why are they so persistent?) that give meaning to our lives. But I suppose a defense of appearance against reality, of a life sustained by a web of illusions, of the bliss of ignorance must seem perverse. People will continue to come to us for what they think of as the truth, even though wisdom might prescribe a healing illusion. The truth, of course, may make *us* free. But freedom is the bane of the ignorant.

But to come to the main point. This entire story seems designed to illustrate the horrors of the state of cognitive anarchy in which we are living. From beginning to end we are presented with difficulties created by folly and misunderstanding, by strange credulity, by undisciplined curiosity, by foolish cleverness. The desire to probe, to discover, to know, to satisfy curiosity, to get the facts so that we can decide better what to do—that is surely a deep hunger of the mind. But we need some restraint in appeasing this hunger, some law, some order. Certainly Laius and Oedipus, father and son, seemed to have in common a voracious ungoverned appetite that did them in. But let me begin at the beginning. With the Sphinx.

There is heavy irony in the story that Oedipus saved the city by driving away or conquering the Sphinx. What truth lies buried in that fable? The city was living through an ordeal with a dreaded questioner; it was being tormented by questions. Anyone going about his business in the streets of the city might be seized by the lapel and subjected to an inquisition that left him speechless, bewildered, confused, crushed. Stopped, soul searched, declared worthless, left deflated, destroyed. If I were permitted an anachronism I would say that this is a cruder version of what the Athenians were subjected to by Socrates. Athens, too, was to get rid of its dreaded questioner, but are we to regard those responsible for putting Socrates to death as the heroes who saved Athens? Socrates compared himself to a gadfly. Can we not consider Oedipus as the one who succeeded in swatting the great Theban gadfly? And, of course, saving Thebes from the stinging questions that might have stirred it to life-saving reflection? Oedipus is the "hero" who put an end to questioning. He was the man who had all the answers. Perhaps I had better say that Oedipus put an end to a certain kind of question, since, as we know, he had plenty of his own to ask and was, in his own way, a ruthless cross-examiner. But there are questions and questions. Some that seek a missing piece in a mosaic; some that lead us into deeper reflective activity in a search for understanding. Where were you on the night of the last full moon and what did you do with the baby? Or, there is a great beast that crawls, strides, hobbles—do you recognize it? Questioning, as we, to whom all come with questions, well know, is a great and complex art—a necessary art, a dangerous art. We can not simply accept the popular view that Oedipus in driving out the Theban questioner really saved the city. He doomed it to continuing folly; it went its way unquestioningly.

And consider the strange case of curiosity about the future. Of course much of our action can be seen as the attempt to avoid or to bring about some state of affairs in the future. If we think we will get sick if we drink too much, we may avoid drinking too much. If we think we will feel better if we lose weight, we may diet. That seems to be what acting intelligently means—considering what will be the case if or unless something is done, and acting to avoid the evil or to achieve the good. And yet, as our candidate points out, there is something utterly absurd in taking a supposed glimpse of the future as justifying infanticide as "self-defense." There is something wrong with calling Laius' action "intelligent," but how is it to be distinguished from other cases of taking the future into consideration? Can we distinguish between acting on a rule confirmed by experience and assumed to hold in the future as it has in the past—like, for example, drinking too much makes you sick—and acting on the belief that one has somehow been given a privileged glimpse of a particular future event? One must rely on experience and be guided by the rules which are its fruits; we cannot rely on supposed revelations about a particular event in the future. Who has such revelations? I suppose that our simple clients confuse the product of our wisdom with a special revelation granted us because of our divine connections. Both Laius and Oedipus seem to have confused general wisdom with "inside information." It is one thing to be reminded that fathers and sons may have deep conflicts that, under some circumstances, might prove fatal; not a divine hint, Laius, that your son is going to kill you unless you kill him first. Yes, Oedipus, sons may strive with fathers and love their mothers; that does not mean you are doomed to kill your father and marry your mother.

But if trying to glimpse the future is full of hazards, what about probing the past? Again we meet difficulties. Who can deny that wisdom grows out of experience, nourished by the memory of things past. Without memory the mind is always naked; to ignore the past is folly. And yet, can we deny that sometimes the digging up of the past is also folly, yielding not wisdom but scandal and pain? Are not some things better buried than revealed, healed by oblivion?

So there it is. The pursuit of knowledge is both necessary and dangerous. The posing of questions, the peering into the future, the digging into the past—done properly, we are nourished; done foolishly, we court disaster.

Need I point out that this defines the problem for us at Delphi? We, if anyone, must be concerned with the correct use of the energies of the mind, with the arts of questioning and answering, with the direction and control of curiosity, with propriety in the pursuit of knowledge. We have made a beginning, but only a beginning. We make mistakes, but we can learn from them.

I suggest that the story of poor Oedipus would make an excellent introductory text—dramatic, enigmatic, raising all the right questions. Perhaps we should ask the candidate whose report I just read to rework the story for that purpose. Perhaps we can find someone else to tell it properly . . . .

Letters From Thebes

LETTER I

It was a bad day for Creon. His son died. His wife died. Both suicides—cursing him. His policy had been a disaster and he had a premonition of it before the blows fell. He was even heard to say—Creon! The great reformer!—that it's probably better to stick to the traditional ways, the ancient laws. But his enlightenment was a bit belated. Exit Creon, crushed . . . .

I did have, as you say, a privileged view of the whole thing. I had been visiting Thebes when the attack came; I had known the central figures since childhood; and everyone seemed eager to tell me everything, to set the record straight, almost as if they expected me to submit a full report to you. I wandered all over the place, spoke to everyone—"in confidence"—and probably do know more of what happened than anyone else. And you insist on a report. If I had the talent I'd try to write

99

a play about it, but you will have to settle for these letters.

I'm not sure I understand you when you caution that you want more than an account of what happened, that you want to know what "really" happened. What happened is that a stubborn girl sprinkled a handful of dust over a rotting corpse and, shortly after, she committed suicide and then her fiance killed himself and then his mother killed herself and then Creon resigned and was led away in shock. All that happened. I don't suppose you want me to fill in the gaps with more "and thens" . . . it would neither entertain nor edify you. Your "really happened" must be a request that I speculate about motives which, you have taught me—or tried to—we can never be certain about, and that you even want me to pass judgement on character and morals and, perhaps, to throw in an analysis of the relation between politics and religion, the will of the king and the will of Zeus and all that. In short, you want an account of what happened, distorted by imagination and prejudice. I will do my best. But now I must stop. Dinner with Ismene. The archetypal survivor, and one of my best sources. To be continued . . . .

LETTER II

Creon's decree is probably the place to begin although, as you once said, every beginning is the end of a long story. The decree, at least, opens the last chapter of the long story that goes back to the days when the young Oedipus drove out the great Theban gadfly, the Sphinx, and, having already killed his own father, married his own mother and settled down to rule a city that, with a sigh of relief, subsided into the pleasures of the unquestioning life. "Leave it alone" is a well-known Theban motto that Oedipus, to his ultimate undoing, failed to respect. Creon, Oedipus' uncle or brother-in-law or both, did not, like a true son of Thebes, take kindly to having his views questioned. He seemed to think that you should think about a problem *before* you decided what to do and then you should act decisively without allowing yourself to be distracted or weakened by doubts or questions. I'm sure you are shaking your head in amused despair. Of course Creon had it all wrong. You and I believe that we never really know enough about the consequences of an act to justify doing it, that decisions ought to be avoided if possible, that when you must decide you should follow your instincts, and that you should only use your "reason" to clean up the mess you make as you go along. Poor Creon. "Think; decide; stand firm." Doomed! But I had better impose some order on this account.

Blind old Oedipus dies in exile. His two daughters, Antigone and Ismene, are now in Thebes. And his two sons, Eteocles and Polynices, fought bitterly over who would rule Thebes, both impartially cursed by the dying old man. Eteocles drove Polynices out; but Polynices returned with an invading force and there was an attempt to storm the city. The attempt failed, but the two brothers killed each other, as their father had hopefully predicted, at one of the great gates of Thebes. Creon took over. He had the best claim to the throne, and he began to pick up the pieces in the still-dazed, grieving, weary, tense, divided, apprehensive city.

Have I given the impression that all this is just a family quarrel? That is part of it, but certainly not the whole story. As someone has said, every city is two cities—a city of the rich and a city of the poor. The brothers put themselves at the head of the opposing factions or parties and the brotherly conflict grew into the familiar Greek civil war between the party of the people and the party of money, the party of change and the party of the good old ways, the radicals and the conservatives. Which brother led which? Does it matter? Why do you want to know? So you can tell the heroes from the villains? So you will know who deserves your support, who you should make excuses for? Well, Eteocles was the leader of the popular party; Polynices was the leader of the rich and aristocratic. And Creon, who was now the ruler of "the city," was also the leader of the democratic, the popular party. It is important to realize that Creon took over during a mere lull in a civil war. Very little had been settled. People had been killed, but factions lived on. Peace had not really arrived. Creon's task, as he saw it, was to consolidate victory, to create some civic unity in the face of internal factionalism and some civic loyalty in the face of a renewed threat of external invasion. He thought about it, alas, and came up with a bright idea. He would make a law!

LETTER III

"Issues!" Creon exploded. "They don't care about issues; they are only looking for pretexts!" He had been telling me about the decree he was planning to announce and I had timidly suggested that he was handing his enemies an issue they could use against him. "It doesn't matter what I do, they'll stir up trouble." He paced restlessly, gesticulating, analyzing the problem as much for himself as for me. Civic loyalty was his obsession. He thought he could handle class conflict within the city. "But when they run off to get military aid from other cities and bring foreign troops in to fight us!" It was treason, he fumed, plain treason. But the aristocrats didn't care. One of them was heard to say that if he had to chose between betraying his city and betraying a friend—a member of his circle—he would, of course, betray his city. Shameless, full of contempt for the rabble, not to be trusted. They needed to be taught a lesson, a simple but important lesson, the difference between a hero and a traitor . . . on and on he went.

It slowly dawned on me that our old friend Creon, now that he was wearing the crown, was trying to take the broad view of things, the statesman's view. City above party! City before friends, before family. Patriots above traitors! He had decided to make an object lesson of Polynices. Eteocles, the loyal brother would be given a hero's funeral. But Polynices, Creon decreed, was to remain unburied, without notice, without honor, without ceremony, deprived of all human rites. Violation of this decree was to be punished by death.

"No one can really disagree with your objectives," I offered pompously, seeing that he had calmed down a bit, "but don't you think your rather extreme methods might be counter-productive? Wouldn't the contrast between a hero's funeral and a quiet burial make the point, without offending people who think everyone is entitled to be buried? Why hand your enemies a religious issue . . ." But here, as I said, he exploded into his tirade.

"You don't understand these people," he went on. "They never quit; they don't appreciate generosity; if you compromise they think you are weak and close in for the kill. If I allowed a simple burial they would give 'simple' a new meaning. No, I'm going to keep it really simple. No tears for Polynices. Not a handful of dust. No burial. Period!"

And that, my friend, is how it began. Creon laid down the law, determined to take a hard line against disloyalty. He had yet to learn that the world conspires to pull the rug out from under the feet of anyone who tries to take a firm stand.

LETTER IV

If you like high-minded, noble, independent, intelligent, virtuous young women you will love Antigone. I detest her. I confess this so that you can discount whatever I say about her. Mine is a distinctly minority opinion, but I don't think of her as noble, or admirable, or "principled," or any other of those things that maudlin sentimentalists are saying about her. I admit that she almost single-handedly pulled off a counter-revolution or, if you think that is a bit strong, at least caused the fall of the people's government. But you don't have to be a nice person to do that sort of thing. I am beginning to wonder if there is not something wrong with those people who are always taking their stand on "principle"—if that is what Antigone did. But I'm getting ahead of the story.

Ismene tells me that Antigone came to see her early, the day after the big battle. She brought news of Creon's edict, and she had not come to discuss it. There was nothing to discuss; she was going to bury Polynices. Nothing was going to stop her—not Creon, not the law, not the death penalty. Would she join her?

"I was shocked," Ismene continued, "and tried to talk her out of it." She paused, stared at the ground, shook her head wearily. "No, I didn't really try to talk her out of it. I knew that was hopeless. I've never talked Antigone out of anything. I just explained why I wouldn't join her. The family had had enough trouble, we were the last ones left, we wouldn't get away with it, it was no disgrace to bow to compulsion, for the weak to submit to the strong. These seemed good enough reasons to me but they did not impress Antigone."

"Don't then," she said scornfully, "if that's the way you feel, I don't want your help. Play it safe, as usual. But I'd rather die than go on living like a coward."

Ismene had little more to add. She had urged caution, but Antigone scorned that too and strode off to meet her destiny. Strange how different the two sisters are. Ismene is clearly the more sensible but Antigone always had the knack of making her feel guilty. Ismene agonized, wept, and survived.

LETTER V

I would prefer to tell this in my own way, but, typically, you fire off a question as if I won't cover some significant point unless you insist on it. Stop tapping your toe impatiently. It only makes me want to slow down.

"What about public opinion?" you ask. I will pretend I know what you mean. So far as I can tell, there was very little enthusiasm for the law from the beginning. Creon was, I know, quite disappointed. He had gone to a lot of trouble about his speech announcing the edict, and it was very good—of its kind. A "ship of state" speech. You know—only when the ship sails steadily can the passengers have a decent voyage; friendship is only possible when you are not seasick, and so on. I'm being unfair. It really was a very good speech. So why do I almost automatically make fun of it? Because I—like you—am the sort of snobbish aristocrat created in order to make Creon's life miserable, just by our habit of sneering at the banal expression of important truths. We are uneasy about patriotism, about civic loyalty, about the need for some unity to override our factionalism—the "diversity" we love, especially our own. We like to mock what we depend on. We blush if we are accused

104

of loving our country. The proper object of loyalty, we think, is the clique . . . .

Creon, as I said, made his speech and announced the decree about not burying Polynices. No wild cheers. "Whatever you say, sir," said the spokesman, "You're the king, and you can give orders to the living and the dead." I thought it a cool—and rather strange—response, and Creon seemed disconcerted. "See that it is carried out," he muttered lamely, turning to leave with all the elan of a man whose speech had just fallen flat. "Oh, sir," the spokesman persisted, "can't you get some younger men to do that?" "I've already assigned guards," said Creon. "Then what is there for us to do?" "Just," growled Creon, "don't support anyone who disobeys." "No one is so stupid as to want to die!" said the spokesman. "But some," concluded Creon with a grim look, "would risk life for money."

An ominous exchange, is it not? Not one expression of support, no endorsement of the policy. "Public opinion," since you ask about that, was no comfort to Creon. The state of affairs that made him think that some "loyalty" law was needed was the same state of affairs that made it easy for him to see conspiracies everywhere. After all, Polynices had brought foreign armies to attack the city, and he did have rich supporters on the inside, still bitter. The elders did give the edict a chilly reception. And that episode with the guards! What episode, you will ask.

No sooner had Creon said that he had assigned guards to the corpse than in stumbled a hapless lout—a guard with bad news. One of those rustic clowns or bumpkin wits so good at making us laugh at things that aren't really funny. With an elaborate story about how he really didn't want to come with bad news, but he had pulled the short straw, and it really wasn't anyone's fault, and they had kept a sharp look-out, and there were no signs of an intruder, and so on. Somehow, ashes had gotten themselves sprinkled over the body, and no one knew how it had happened.

Before the incredulous Creon could even react to the unlikely story the old spokesman, with surprising alacrity, offered his contribution. "Sir," he said "it occurs to me that perhaps we can see the hand of god in this?"

Creon brushed aside the religious hypothesis. The gods, he declared flatly, do not honor villains and traitors who come here to destroy our temples and overturn our laws. This is not an act of god; it is an act of money! Someone was bribed! And he launched into a powerful diatribe against the corrupting effect of money. "Of all the vile things on earth, nothing is as vile as money . . .!" He went on in this vein, speaking out of deep conviction and, I thought, with some accuracy. Finally, he ordered the guard off, with dire threats, to find the criminal.

I had a quick word with Creon shortly after this scene. He was alone, lying down, massaging his brow. I murmured something he must have taken as an expression of sympathy— and it may have been. "Let me tell you something, young man," sitting up wearily, "The trouble with being the leader of the people is that your followers are stupid and incompetent. You collect aphorisms—write that down—I give you permission. Unhappy the leader whose followers are stupid. Unhappy the leader of the people. Something like that!" He dismissed me with a wave of the hand.

LETTER VI

"If there is anything I can't stand," Creon was speaking, and it was the next day and, it seemed, a different world, "if there is anything I can't stand, it is people who look down on politics, who don't care about local government, who don't know where city hall is, utterly indifferent to the details of practical affairs, who just think they happen to know all about what goes on in heaven. Zeus says do this, don't do that, the gods want this, they say you shouldn't do that, there's an eternal ordinance covering that point. They know all about the other world and nothing of this one. They are beyond reason, unmovable, self-righteous, irresponsible, and utterly attractive to idiots." He glanced at me, looking for agreement. As I've said, I don't like Antigone either, but I didn't think Creon needed encouragement. I tried not to nod.

You will gather that things have happened since my last letter. They caught Antigone. The relieved guards brought her

106

before Creon and she not only admitted that she had done it but admitted—admitted isn't quite the right word for "boldly asserted"—that she knew she was violating the edict. How did she dare! Creon wanted to know. Her answer has had the town buzzing. Everywhere you go you see small groups deep in argument, red-faced citizens, arms waving, voices rising, stalking off in rage. And what are they arguing about? The laws of heaven!

Yes, the laws of heaven. "Unwritten, unchanging, eternal" Antigone called them. She would obey them, not Creon's edict. She didn't care about dying; she would have to die sometime and she thought life—her life, anyway—a miserable business. But she didn't want to offend the gods by defying them, by breaking their laws. Creon could do whatever he wanted. She would obey the gods. That's why she buried her brother. That was the line she took.

I'm not sure what annoyed Creon more: that she had committed the crime or that, as he said, "she tried to glorify the crime as a virtue." He seemed to have no doubts on either score. It was utterly clear to him that you did not treat a hero and a traitor the same way. "Good" and "bad" were more fundamental than "relative"—even "brother." "These old family ties," Creon fumed. "The fact that he was her brother was supposed to outweigh the fact that he was a traitor. I'm not going to coddle aristocrats who play fast and loose with the city, who treat it as one of their nursery toys. The edict was a good idea!"

But the laws of heaven! Creon threw up his hands. "Ruling is hard enough in any case," he said. "In the old days people at least thought that if the king made a law you were supposed to obey it. Not that everyone always did, but you understood that you were supposed to. But now! You don't have to obey the king's law if it doesn't agree with what you think is the law of heaven!"

"I really don't mind an honest law-breaker. What I can't stand is someone who claims a *right* to break the law." Creon was warming up to his text. "Sorry, King, I've decided to obey the gods instead of you. So then I say, of course! Let's all obey the gods! Just show me god's law, a copy of the laws of heaven. Sorry, she says, its not written down. Its just been there all the time, from eternity. And you're sure it says you should bury your traitor brother? I have made a vulgar remark. Of course, she says coolly, we've always buried brothers in our family, and I'm sure the gods like it that way. The higher law, you see; the law for high-brows; the eternal law; the way we've always done things. Tradition! Ahah!" Creon pounced. Tradition, custom, the old ways, always the old ways, the eternal proprieties, the ancient proprietors—that, explained Creon, is what the eternal law of the heavens comes down to. The old order. Polynices' people. Money. And priests, don't forget the priests. Servile frauds, paid prophets. "I know them," he said, "I've done my share of traveling to Delphi, and I know them all. But don't let me get started on *that* ..."

There was an anti-clerical streak in Creon as well as a loathing for the old aristocracy and a deep suspicion of the power of money—quite apparent even before everything closed in on him. He didn't trust the priests, the aristocrats, the rich. So who could he count on? The "ignorant masses" who, he asked wryly, were credulous, superstitious, and, always broke, easily bribed? He was not at home with those he led. He was, in fact, a lonely figure, not close to anyone, rather loveless. Except ... except for the apple of his eye, his comfort, his pride, his hope for the future, his son, Haemon.

LETTER VII

I think that what really broke Creon—although it didn't show at the time—was his clash with his son. He never changed his mind about Antigone although, at the end, he was going to set her free. But the argument with her only hardened his resolve. And I can't believe that old Tiresias brought him around or scared him into relenting, although Creon was willing to let it appear that way. No, it was Haemon. I'm sure you will savor the irony. Poor Creon, struggling to elevate civic duty, civic loyalty, above narrower family ties—trying to teach Thebes that that was the key to its salvation. And suddenly, there is his son pleading the case of a criminal because he would like to marry her. What was Creon to do? He did the only thing he could: he lost his temper.

But I had better describe the whole scene. Ismene, pleading ineffectively—first with Antigone, to be allowed to share responsibility for the illegal burial, and then with Creon for mercy for Antigone (how can I live without my sister?)—brought up the delicate subject. Are you really going to execute the girl your son wants to marry? Creon did not actually say that preventing the marriage was one good thing Antigone's lawlessness had achieved, but for a moment I thought he'd say it.

"There are other girls in Thebes. Haemon can have his pick," he growled. "But," pleaded Ismene, "they are so much in love!" "My son," he said flatly, "is not going to marry an evil woman. Take her away!" And he braced himself for the inevitable showdown with his son. Which came promptly. Enter Haemon.

"My son," Creon went right to the point, "I've sentenced Antigone to death. I suppose you've heard. The sentence is irreversible. Now, are you going to support me or are you going to throw a tantrum?"

You would have admired young Haemon. He was seething, but he had enough self-control to pull off one of the most insincere speeches on record. "Father, you are wiser than I am. My marriage isn't as important as being guided by your wisdom." It was a brilliant opening move.

Reassured, Creon delivers a speech. How good it is to have children who are loyal and obedient. How terrible it would be to have a wicked, disloyal, disobedient wife—disobedient as Antigone has shown herself to be. How if he wants to encourage obedience generally, he must insist on it in his own family. Obedience to the law! Respect for authority! All that stands between us and civil strife and chaos—vintage Creon. But there were two things I noticed that would, I'm sure, interest you. First, when Creon lauds respect for authority he does not mean only that you should respect or obey any law you believe is right or just, that you think "worthy" of respect.

Any fool holds that! Creon means *real* respect—you obey any law, just or unjust. You don't pick and choose. You act out of respect, not on your own judgment. And second, Creon seems obsessed by the prospect of being beaten by a woman. It is not just that he dislikes and fears Antigone—scary and detestable as she can be. It seems to be more general. As if Creon sees "femininity" as the enemy of authority, respect, civility and all that. There is a fight for Haemon's soul between Creon and order and "that girl," softness, sentiment, chaos; between manliness and the womanly.

Now it is Haemon's turn. He is not, he says, going to presume to try to refute his father. But as a loyal son he will tell him what others are afraid to tell him. He, Haemon, gets around and hears all the rumors and gossip. And what he hears is that Antigone has lots of sympathy and support. For burying her brother, people say, she should be rewarded, not punished. Creon's sentence is very unpopular, and Haemon is worried about his father's reputation.

You will note that there is no attempt to meet Creon on his own ground, to discuss loyalty or unity or obedience to law or the needs of a distracted city torn by civil war. Perhaps someday in the distant future we will have intelligent discussions of the merits of decisions instead of these samplings of gossip, rumor, or unenlightened popular opinion—but not in these degenerate times.

But Haemon is not finished. Having informed Creon that what he is doing is unpopular he goes on to deliver a lecture about "rigidity"—about trees that snap if they don't bend, and boats that overturn if you don't slacken the sheet. In short, Creon should relax, relent, change his decision, compromise. It was an Ismene-like speech in defense of an uncompromising Antigone, a speech Antigone would have detested, an old man's speech in the mouth of an ardent young suitor. And, of course, it did not move Creon who comments ironically about youth instructing age. Forget my age, snaps Haemon, it's what I do that counts. Like defending criminals? says Creon. Public opinion doesn't consider her a criminal, Haemon retorts. Is public opinion the ruler or am I, asks Creon. Talk about being childish! sneers Haemon. And you are not ashamed of quarreling with your father? Not when you are unjust and trample on religion!

Finally! So much for self-restraint! I can't respect you when you are unjust and trample on religion! Creon has had enough. "You are not going to marry the girl. She is going to die." "If she dies," rages Haemon, "she won't die alone. And you'll never see me again." Off he goes.

Do I think that Haemon was really concerned, as he claimed, about his father's political standing? No, I don't. He simply wanted the king, his father, to let the woman he adored go free. The will, or whim, of Aphrodite no doubt. The highest law. Of course it would be expecting too much to expect young Haemon to realize that what he was asking was impossible. Can you imagine a speech by Creon explaining why he was letting Antigone go free? "My son tells me that in the circles he moves in—Antigone's aristocratic friends—she is regarded as a heroine for defying the law and honoring her traitor-brother. Of course I didn't mean that the edict should apply to *her*; she's practically a member of my own family. But no one else . . .!"

No, impossible; and Creon knew it. Although he may not have known how to handle his son with tact. But now that I think of it, how do you handle Haemon if you are not simply going to do what he wants? No matter how you put it, he is not going to take no for an answer. "She won't be the only one to die!" and "You'll never see me again!" are almost inevitable exit lines for him . . . .

LETTER VIII

Well, you were wrong. Antigone did not go quietly and with dignity into that dark cave. Did you expect her to skip the swan song? It would be churlish to begrudge her a long last word, but I heard it, nevertheless, unmoved. All that earlier scorn for Ismene for wanting to go on living, that talk of death as a welcome relief—not today. Now it is poor Antigone who will never know the joys of marriage, poor Antigone ruined by her miserable family, poor Antigone going to her doom all alone. And poor Antigone with a new argument about why she had to do it. She would not have disobeyed the law, have set herself in defiance of the city, to bury a mere husband; she could always find another husband. Nor, she says, to bury her children, if she had any; she could always have more children. But since her parents were dead she could never have another brother, so she had to bury her uniquely irreplaceable brother. Oh well, I can't blame her for being distracted. It was a day for non sequiturs. She was still protesting, as they led her away, that she had not violated any of heaven's laws.

LETTER IX

The question of loyalty to the city had become a fuss about a requiem for a traitor and then an argument about disobedience and the higher law and then a problem of family favoritism and compromise. Creon seemed to be the only one who cared about the big issue. Everyone else had more particular concerns—a brother, a sister, a sweetheart. That, I suppose, is why it is so easy to dislike Creon. He held aloft the banner of the city, declared himself the defender of the principle of civic unity and law, dared to affirm the necessity of loyalty and, unlike the ordinary politician, expected even his relatives to obey the law. A public-spirited man in a self-centered, self-indulgent world, a lone adult in a world of children.

LETTER X

"It was like a bad dream, a nightmare," he spoke slowly, thoughtfully, without a trace of passion. It was some days after the debacle and I was surprised to see him looking so well. They had led him away, utterly crushed, moaning that it was all his fault. Now, when his old servant let me in to see him—I knew you'd want Creon's side of the story—he was reclining, actually making notes. It was the first time I'd seen him that he didn't look worried. There, I thought, is a man without a care in the world, with absolutely nothing more to lose. He was, of course, no longer in office and was without a family to fret about. Alone, relieved of all burdens. "Carefree" popped into my mind. Inappropriate, I thought; but I couldn't shake the feeling. He looked carefree. Not quite cheerful, but not plagued by guilt either.

"A bad dream," he repeated, waving me to a chair. "Those kids! Antigone panicking, beginning to sing a different tune. And Haemon, threatening, as he often did when he didn't get his way, to run away from home . . ." He paused. "I had arranged to have Antigone shut up in a cave, with some food. I would have found some pretext for letting her out in a few days . . ." I stared. Did he expect me to believe that? That he had not intended to go through with the death sentence?

He shot me a quick glance, as if to see how I was taking this version of recent events, hesitated, continued. "That fraud, Tiresias, gave me the perfect pretext. Dire omens! Threats of disaster! I stood up to him and he stalked off in a cloud of curses." I am not superstitious, but I could see that he had scared the wits out of the people who were listening. He's never been wrong, the spokesman quavered. So I pretended to be frightened after all. "What should I do," I said, "I'll do whatever you say, whatever the people want." And they told me to free Antigone and build a tomb for Polynices. "All right," I agreed, "let's do it."

"But it was too late. Antigone was in a hurry to die and had hanged herself. I didn't kill her. It was suicide. And she drove poor Haemon out of his mind." He fell silent for a moment, brooding. "She was the wrong girl for him, never did him any good. Snobbish, cold, too complicated. Not like Ismene. That's the one he should have married. But bad marriages are an old story with us. One way or another, Antigone would have destroyed Haemon. So she hanged herself and pushed him over the edge; he killed himself at her feet. And when his mother heard about it, she killed herself too. Three suicides in one day! At first I blamed myself, but now I see that it wasn't really my fault. Still, its not easy to get rid of irrational guilt feelings . . ."

I found this a bit hard to take, so I tried to change the subject.

113

Didn't he think that Tiresias had really raised some significant points? Even Antigone? Wasn't there something to the law of heaven argument? Could the king expect obedience if he ordered his subjects to do something against the will of the gods?

"Ah," he said, "I didn't know you were one of these new-style higher-law theorists. As it happens, I've been giving the matter some thought and I wouldn't mind discussing it with someone who isn't a priest or a fool. Why don't you stay for dinner?" I accepted the invitation, of course. In my next letter I will tell you what Creon thinks about it all.

LETTER XI

"You don't really understand the point of authority," said Creon, "until you've experienced chaos or civil war." He had had several cups of wine, but he spoke clearly. "Then you realize that its not a luxury but a deep necessity. People are bound to quarrel and soon they are ready to kill each other—for an insult, a trifle, an idea. Someone has to stop it, and he can't stop it just by being wise or right. The foolish and wicked are not impressed by wisdom and virtue. The only thing that works is the assertion of authority—the ruler's edict, backed by awe, fear, respect. Do this! he says. And everyone stops fighting and obeys. Not because everyone thinks he is right, not because they agree with the ruler, but just because the ruler says so."

"Surely you can't mean that," I interrupted as he paused for a sip, "surely you must mean that the ruler is just and that we subjects must respect justice . . ." He didn't let me finish. "Don't be silly. When did you see a ruler who understood justice or practiced it? No, you can't have peace if you teach people to follow justice, only if you teach them to follow their ruler. To respect the ruler, to do what he says, not to argue with him, or try to score points or show that you are more sensitive or perceptive than he is. I don't claim to be infallible about justice or wisdom, but who is? A headstrong, badly brought-up girl like Antigone spoiled by a cleverly idiotic father? Or a venal old omen-mongering priest? Or . . .," he favored me with an ironic bow, "a supercilious, sophisticated playboy like you?" I hastened to assure Creon that I knew very little about justice or virtue or wisdom. He did not treat my confession as a startling revelation.

Creon went on in this vein for some time, wandering around the point, repetitive, heavy, assertive. I was puzzled by a haunting sense of familiarity until it dawned on me that he was a clumsy caricature of *you*. The manner was altogether different, of course, but he was saying—without your elegance and eloquence—what you always say: that we can never be certain that we are right about what to do; that men are incurably combative; that salvation lies in the habit of respect, easily destroyed by the habit of irreverent questioning. So now you can see what happens when your ideas find refuge in the mind of a . . . of a Creon.

"What about the law of heaven, the will of the gods?" I prodded when he began to slow down. He stared at me. "We're alone now. You don't have to pretend. Don't tell me you're a believer in Tiresian mumbo-jumbo? . . ." I shook my head in hasty denial.

"What you really mean is, do I, King Creon, believe in what my peasants believe," he paused long enough for me to hurriedly shake my head, "and if not, what is there to keep me from doing stupid or evil things. What will restrain me if not the fear of heaven?" That's it, I nodded.

"First," he said, as if he knew he had a lot to say, "We can't help it, you and I, if we don't happen to believe what some people think it would be useful for us to believe. It's not my fault that it isn't true. So a figure of speech like Zeus isn't going to keep me from being oppressive, if that's my inclination. But second, let's suppose there is a law of heaven. Who is more likely to know what it is? The king or one of his subjects? If Zeus made me king it stands to reason he'd see to it that I'd know what I was supposed to know about what he wants. He'd hardly tell Antigone and leave me in the dark about it. And third . . .," now he needed another point. His eyes wandered, then lit up. "And third, do you think he'd tell it to the birds who would tell it an old freak like Tiresias (he didn't seem to like Tiresias) who would come tottering along to tell it to me? Is that the way deity communicates with royalty? Through crackpots and frauds?"

Well, that was Creon's argument about the higher law. No such thing. And if there was, neither subjects nor priests were likely to know any more about it than the duly anointed king. It amused me to think of you putting the same argument in the "philosophical" terms you love—fancier, but no clearer.

It was quite late when I succeeded in getting to the door. "Oh wait!" he called after me. "You wanted to know what could restrain me." I waited. "The fear of annoying a lot of people. They'd get rid of me. That's my rule. Don't annoy them. Don't stir them up." He stood up. A lonely pathetic figure. "Except this time," he spoke wistfully. "This time I ignored my rule. I thought it was an emergency. I tried to do the right thing, to be the savior of the city, a statesman, not a politician. Look where it got me . . ." He shrugged and turned away. It was the last time I saw him.

LETTER XII

I don't appreciate your lack of appreciation. I was sure you'd like my last letters—a crisp account of what happened, a discussion of the salient issues, a bit of poetic license, and even an exclusive interview with Creon. And what is my reward? "Too much Creon, surely?" And whose story do you think it is, if not Creon's? The star-crossed young lovers? The bumbling priest? The family feud? What is interesting about a high-minded young woman who elevates her whim into a divine law and courts martyrdom, or about a young man who is furious because he can't talk his father into pardoning his enemy? They have no problems, only passions lightly dusted with principles. But Creon! There is a man with *problems*! The only one concerned with the public good, with everyone against him, picking on him, wanting something from him. The fact is, he's the only one worth thinking about. It's his story.

I've been too sympathetic, have I? Do you want me to turn him into a blundering brute? Because that's how you like to think of populist leaders? Well, I'm not writing to reinforce your prejudices. He is neither dolt nor brute. Impatient, but with a lot to be impatient about. I tried to give him his due.

But I know what's bothering you. You write that all our friends are making a hero out of Antigone, that they are all buzzing about something they are calling "civil disobedience." She is your darling because she defied the law in the name of the higher law. And if she is the hero then Creon has to be the villain. And I didn't tailor Creon to that role. So you grumble.

I presume now to advise you. Don't go overboard about "civil disobedience." Praise Antigone, if you want to. Contribute to the Polynices Memorial Fund. Support our Aristocratic party wherever you can. That's honest partisan politics of the sort we've always practiced. But don't make a fetish of civil disobedience or treat it as a thing to be applauded. For one very good reason. You need to know who is doing it to whom. Imagine that Polynices had won, had forbidden honors to that radical, Eteocles, that Haemon or some other young zealot had defied the law, had practiced civil disobedience to summon up support for that subversive egalitarian—against *us*. Would you and our friends then swoon over civil disobedience? Of course not. It's not a principle that commands respect by itself. When we do it it's idealism; when they do it it's a crime. So even though all good conservatives will drink a toast to Antigone, let us do so because she is on our side, not because she was disobedient. To a good aristocratic girl who destroyed a strong democratic ruler!

But I will stop trying to advise you. Advice, as you once said, is a futile comment on the course of events. So no more letters. I will be leaving Thebes soon, before the next attack I hope. This place is now a doomed shamble of factions. I suppose, when you think of Thebes, you will think of Antigone. I will think of Creon. And I will think of him as a harassed man with family problems who was just trying to do his job and was, alas, crushed by the burden of office.

117

Moses

The flight from Egypt is not the first great departure story in the Bible. There was an earlier dramatic exodus from Eden—that blissful land whose memory haunts all promised lands. It too was a final parting of the ways, a movement towards a hazardous autonomy, toward freedom and responsibility. But Egypt was not Eden, and the differences dwarf resemblance. Slaves in Egypt; innocents in Paradise. But from both conditions and from both places there stretches a perilous journey towards a dimly seen goal.

Moses was the leader of the great escape, the break-out, the flight, the long march that created the Jews. It was a flight from oppression, not a struggle to overthrow the oppressors, to turn the tables on them. It was not a rebellion or a revolution as we ordinarily think of them. But it was a liberation movement, and Moses was its leader—out of bondage, through the desert, to the promised land . . . .

It is a bit early to call them Jews. They were not yet the people of The Book. It is really difficult to get any sense of what they were like, except that they were to reveal, quite soon, a taste for black humor and a quickness to complain. There is nothing terribly attractive about them, nor are we told that they were especially good at anything, nor obviously marked for any special destiny. But there were a great many of them and they were worked very hard.

They were in Egypt, but they were not regarded as real Egyptians even though they had been there for something like four hundred years. Their arrival in the dim past—four hundred years!—had been part of the restless wandering of nomadic tribes driven or attracted to Egypt to escape famine. Tradition had it that one of their great ancestors, Joseph, had risen high in the service of Egypt and was associated with a basic change in the pattern of land ownership that had greatly strengthened the power of Pharaoh. Joseph's kin had enjoyed royal favor then, had settled down in Egypt, but clung to a semi-pastoral way of life. Time passed and, as it is said, there came a pharaoh who knew not Joseph. A pharaoh who, when he thought of Joseph's kin or the descendants of Israel thought of them only as a great problem.

What was the problem? To begin with, the original handful had grown, if we are to trust the text, into hundreds of thousands of lower-class manual laborers, essentially slaves. There must have been cultural or ethnic differences sufficient to account for the fact that they had not been assimilated long ago into the general Egyptian culture. They seem to have settled en masse to the bottom of the social pyramid. Still alien, obviously inferior, clearly unassimilable, an exploited class upon whose cheap labor Egypt depended. They were needed as cheap labor is needed; they were valued and despised, as cheap labor is valued and despised. And they were feared as a power that must be kept under control is feared. In a crisis, there was no reason to expect support or loyalty. Pharaoh put it succinctly. "These Israelites have become too many and too strong for us. We must take precautions to see that they do not increase any further; or we shall find that, if war breaks out, they will join the enemy and fight against us, and they will become masters of the country."

There was no suggestion that an attempt be made to win the hearts and minds of the slaves, that their condition be ameliorated, that they should be given reason to become grateful and loyal. It would be nice to know that somewhere on the fringes of the court a few kindly dreamers spoke softly about the possibility of integrating the oppressed into the happy mainstream of high Egyptian life, that pangs of guilt pierced some tender Egyptian souls. But of such whispers or such pangs the scanty record is silent.

Instead, a harsh two-pronged policy was adopted. The slaves were organized into work-gangs required to fill heavy production quotas and subjected to severe discipline. That is, life was made increasingly onerous. And, a policy of population control was put into effect. All male children were to be killed at birth. But the policy solved nothing. Overworking people did not make them more trustworthy. And the population policy was strangely ineffective. It was sabotaged by Israelite midwives who were supposed to kill the newborn boys; and when Pharaoh authorized any Egyptian to kill a newborn Israelite boy we do not hear that there was an enthusiastic response. A helpless babe was more likely to be adopted than killed even, I think, in Egypt. So the problem remained. What to do with a very large population of exploited, maltreated, disaffected slaves upon whose labor you depended and whose very presence was a menace. Guest-workers who had overstayed their welcome, whom you wouldn't want your daughter to marry, and who had been there so long that it made no sense to say "Israelite! Go back to where you came from!" And whose labor was among your chief assets.

Seen by the Egyptians as a sullen, ominous mass, how did the children of Israel see themselves? We are given few, if any, clues to their inner life. We call them the children of Israel, but we do not know what or how much they thought of the pedigree with which we have provided them. Did they speak of Joseph who had brought them there four centuries ago? Did they know that Israel, Joseph's father, was, presumably, that Jacob who had deceived Isaac and stolen Esau's birthright? Did they know that Isaac had narrowly escaped sacrifice at the hands of his father, Abraham? Did they know and cherish all this, not yet neatly recorded, or were they sunk in an unilluminated weary present, toil-worn, lash-bruised, not knowing who they were nor nourishing dreams of what they were to become. Clearly, there was some sense of identity as a people, as somehow aliens together in Egypt, but the great experience that was to shape their identity still lay ahead of them.

It was into this hopeless situation that Moses was born. The text is clear about who he was—the son of descendants of Levi, one of the sons of Israel. But there has been a good deal of speculation about the legends of the birth of the hero, and this story about an infant rescued from a river is not unique. When Moses first appears to us as an adult he seems to be an Egyptian nobleman, raised as the son of a daughter of Pharaoh, trained in the arts of Egypt. Was the story of the rescued Israelite foundling generally known? Did Moses look Jewish? Or was he thought to be what he seemed to be—except to a few who knew, and perhaps guarded, the secret of his birth? Oddly enough, his adult career is compatible with either view of his origins. On one version he is an Egyptian nobleman who came to side with the oppressed Israelites and undertook to lead them to freedom. On the other version he is an Israelite who was brought up as an Egyptian nobleman and—after the same adventures—undertook to lead his oppressed people to freedom. What is clear in any case is that the great leader of the movement did not emerge from among the oppressed masses, had not made bricks in the sun nor felt the lash, had not struggled to the top of the heap. No one has described Moses, whatever his birth, as a man of the people. When we first meet him on a venture into the Israelite quarter he is something like the young man raised in private schools and an elite college and university who surreptitiously visits the ghetto with which he has some tenuous, undefined connection. He is not one of the local boys.

Moses, we are told, went to see the Israelites at work. He saw an Egyptian, presumably some sort of foreman or supervisor, beat one of the workers. "He looked this way and that, and, seeing there was no one about, he struck the Egyptian down and hid his body in the sand."

I can imagine a conversation that evening among some weary

slaves. "It was a routine beating. And then up steps this man—he was dressed like a rich Egyptian—and hits the foreman over the head with something he was carrying. The foreman falls down dead; the stranger drags him out of the road and covers him with some sand and scoots away. They'll find the body tomorrow. Egyptian foremen don't just disappear. We'll pay for it. What did he think he was doing?" Moses must have thought he was coming to the aid of the oppressed.

The next day Moses returned, saw two slaves (or Israelites or Hebrews) fighting, and tried to intervene to stop it. The Bible is so succinct that it is easier to quote than to paraphrase. "He (Moses) asked the man who was in the wrong, 'why are you striking him?' 'Who set you up as an officer and a judge over us?' the man replied. 'Do you mean to murder me as you murdered the Egyptian?' Moses was alarmed. 'The thing must have become known,' he said to himself. When Pharaoh heard of it, he tried to put Moses to death, but Moses made good his escape and settled in the land of Midian."

It is a breathtaking transformation. One day, an Egyptian nobleman; the next day a visit to the Hebrew neighborhood, a glimpse of brutality, an impulsive killing; the next day rebuffed in his attempt to intervene as a peacemaker in the internal quarrels of some slaves (Egyptian, get lost!) ; by the end of the week, a fugitive from Egyptian justice, a refugee in the land of Midian. Must we not see him as a sheltered aristocrat who means well, who wants to help the downtrodden, who blunders into a rough world he does not understand, whose impulsive action helps no one, whose naive offer of leadership is scornfully rejected, and who, wanted by the police, flees the country. Young beyond his years, unrealistic, ineffectual, well meaning. He had killed for the oppressed! They had rejected him, turned on him, even (someone must have told Pharaoh!) betrayed him. He may have been "trained in all the wisdom of the Egyptians," but he now faced the beginning of a second education.

We are told very little about the next phase of Moses' life. There is the familiar story of gallantry at the well in which he comes to the aid of the daughters of a priest of Midian.

Moses marries one of the daughters, Zipporah, and settles down in Midian, "minding the flock of his father-in-law, Jethro." As we would put it, Moses the refugee marries the daughter of a prominent Midian and goes to work as a foreman of his sheep ranch. We do not know how much time passes—how many years—before, one day, leading his flock along the edge of the wilderness, near what we will call Mt. Sinai, Moses sees the light.

The encounter at the burning bush marks the significant turning point in the life of Moses the exile. He emerges from the experience with a mission, a calling that is to dominate the rest of his life. He is going to return to Egypt—the Israelites are still suffering oppression, but the old pharoah is dead and Moses is probably no longer on the dusty most-wanted list—and rescue the slaves from bondage; he is going to re-settle them in the land of Canaan as a people of a new order, a new morality, a new law of their own.

There is, as we know, a crisis of inspiration, of the turning point, of the moment when what has been a vague subject of prolonged brooding reflection suddenly becomes brightly clear, crystallizes into a plan, a mission. There was such a moment of illumination for Moses, settled into the life of husband and father, working for his father-in-law, tending sheep in a hospitable but alien land. And it ended the idyll.

I cannot believe that the "call" came to Moses out of the blue, from beyond the range of his shepherding speculation, untouched by his experience as the leader of sheep. Who knows what haunted his dreams of the flight from Egypt, of the fate of those he had left toiling without hope in the land of his birth. Who knows how his youthful sympathy reshaped itself, how his ineffectual idealism matured into the habits of purposeful discipline, how his powers developed, how he struggled with his own doubts, how he groped toward his life's plan, illuminated suddenly by the strange glow on a mysterious mountain.

However fate had contrived it, Moses was, by this time, a creature of three cultures. He had been raised as an aristocratic

Egyptian and knew Egypt from the inside. He knew something—although he had not shared in it—of the culture of the slaves. However he may have "belonged" to it, he had, in more than one sense, escaped from it. If he was indeed born a Hebrew, he had passed as an Egyptian and had avoided the usual Hebrew fate. Yet, to some degree, he was aware of, sympathized with, identified himself with the enslaved children of Israel. But his life as an exile had immersed him in yet a third culture—in something like what the children of Israel might have become if they had not made the fateful detour and followed Joseph into Egypt. The Midianites were not Egyptians; they were not Hebrews. They were, apparently, descendants of Abraham who had avoided both Egypt and slavery. It is in this culture that Moses grew to maturity, married and had children, and lived the life of a prosperous raiser of sheep in the shadow of Mt. Sinai. It was a good life. A life, it must often occurred to him, that Hebrews could live if they were not held as slaves in Egypt.

We now see a complex Moses. A man with an Egyptian education, a Hebrew identification, and something of a Midian ideal—a notion of how one might live if freed from bondage, if neither oppressor nor oppressed. So the plan, when it takes shape, does not, as I said, come out of the blue. It comes out of the elements of Moses' life, out of a consciousness that is always outside of whatever it is immersed in, always in part alien to itself, always divided—part Egyptian, part Hebrew, part yearner for an unspoiled promised land, that is, part utopian. He is the first of a line of modern Jews: a master of the magic of the goyim, but uneasy with the establishment; inwardly attached to the ghetto from which he has escaped, to whose culture he is at least partly a stranger; and something of an idealist. A divided self, a wanderer between cultures, yearning for a home of his own.

A time in exile is, as we know, a familiar feature in the life of a great revolutionary leader. In exile, or in prison, removed from the world in which he is ultimately to act, he develops his character, his powers, and his general plan. In Moses' case, the goal was to lead the slaves out of Egypt and settle them in a new Midian of their own, in Canaan. To realize his goal he was to rely on three things. First, he seems, in his mastery of the lore of Egypt, to have become a formidable magician or illusionist with a great many impressive tricks up his sleeve. This art was the least among his assets, of some, but not decisive, utility. Second, he found a right-hand man, a brother or half-brother, Aaron, who could serve as intermediary between Moses and the Hebrews to whom Moses was something of an outsider, a stranger who may not even have mastered their tongue, a cultured alien who had never lived among them. Aaron may well have been an indispensable ally.

But third, and most significantly, Moses harnessed the powerful tide of religious energy rising irresistibly among the oppressed. He returned to Egypt as the instrument of the god of the great patriarchs, the god of the fathers of the Hebrews, the god who remembered them and cherished them and would lead them out of bondage. This was the central feature of Moses' inspiration. He, Moses, did not claim to be the liberator. He was merely the messenger, the tool, the agent of Jehovah the great God who had tested Abraham, who had brought the descendants of Abraham's grandson to Egypt, who now would take them out of Egypt to the promised land. This was not merely the scheme of some Moses or other. It was God's plan.

Thus inspired, thus armed, Moses, well past the middle of the journey of his life, returns to Egypt.

His first task, and not an easy one, is to establish himself with the Israelites as their leader. In what is surely one of the earliest revival meetings on record, Moses "converts" the assembled elders of the Israelites. He brings the message of the old god with the new name who has remembered and renewed the old promise, who will save them and lead them out of bondage. He impresses them with his powers—he does his tricks with snakes and with healing. He brings the promise of salvation, and the hopeless come to life again "and they bowed themselves to the ground in worship."

We know next to nothing of the "religious" life of the Israelites at this point. And it means very little to say that Moses became their religious leader. Were there obscure sacred texts for him to interpret with blinding insight? Were there money-changers to be driven from shrines? A priesthood to be lashed out of sloth? No, not yet. But there must have been something, some memories handed down so that Moses had something to remind them of; some habits of awe, so that they understood that bowing down in worship was a way of responding to a glimmer of hope. They accepted Moses as their leader, and it does no harm to say "religious leader."

It is as religious leader that Moses encounters Pharaoh. His first request is for a holiday so that the Israelites can go into the desert to pay homage to their god. Pharaoh refuses to let an enormous number of slaves stop working in order to worship a god he has never heard of. If that's the sort of thing you are thinking of, he says, you must not be working hard enough. He lays on an additional burden, and the lot of the slaves becomes noticeably harsher. The Israelite foremen turn bitterly on Moses and Moses himself is badly shaken and discouraged by the fruits of his militance. The people are in no mood to listen when he reminds them that he has not come to make things easier for them but to free them from bondage.

The initial conflict is really less between Israelite and Egyptian—Pharaoh has only been annoyed—than between the two factions or tendencies or alternatives that always struggle for dominance in the camp of the oppressed. There are the pragmatists who believe that half a loaf is better than none and that with a bit of luck and patience the half might become two-thirds; and there are the militant idealists who want it all, who are willing to risk everything in the desert for the sake of what may lie beyond it. Moses has not returned from Midian to improve Israelite rations in Egypt. He realized, had been warned, that things would get worse before they could get better. But he was shocked by the harshness of the reality of making bricks without straw, by the immediately painful result of his confident militance, by how quickly things could get worse for slaves who wanted dignity (a religious holiday! What next?).

If I linger over the scene of Moses' remorse about the misery he seems to have increased, his anguished doubt about the course he is taking, his despair in this "dark night of the soul," it is because it is a rare display of sympathy or tenderness by a leader more noted for other qualities than compassion, a display of the humanity whose inevitable deadening was to make him unfit for entry into the promised land. But now Moses, with renewed faith in the inevitability of liberation, resumed the struggle.

THE WAR AGAINST PHARAOH

We now come to the dramatic oft-told story of the conflict between Moses and Pharaoh that ends with the Israelites milling about exultantly in the desert, beyond the reach of Pharaoh's foundered chariots. The refrain "Let my people go!" grows from the initial request for a holiday foray to an implicit but well-understood demand for total liberation. Pharaoh refuses to set his slaves free. Moses persists; Pharaoh, under heavy pressure, stubbornly holds his ground. But in the end, Pharaoh cracks, lets the slaves go, regrets his decision, goes in pursuit, and loses his army. Thus ends a four-hundred year chapter in the history of the children of Israel—the sojourn in Egypt.

Is it Moses who creates the great series of natural disasters that overwhelm Pharaoh? We are not asked to believe that, but we should, at this point, reflect on the notion of the natural disaster as punishment. We do not need to reach back to the story of the Flood, considered as a large scale imposition of capital punishment by a disgusted God, in order to capture or recapture the conception of the natural order as an embodiment of justice. The notion that nature gives you what you deserve is still alive and well among us. If you are greedy about fattening food it serves you right if you get fat; the punishment for smoking is lung cancer. Behave, or else! And if wrong-doing does not immediately hurt the body, is it not supposed to take its toll in the sickening of the soul? The notion of a vigilant nature, counting every calorie, noting every puff, even sending painful monitory warnings before the inevitable summing up of the score of the heedless, is far from dead. Nature has its laws and exacts a natural retribution. How have

I sinned that I should have these boils? complains Job. But this applies also on a larger scale. Let there be a devastating fire and we will hear the warning that if we do not mend our unjust ways we will next have a flood. Let there be an earthquake or an epidemic and there will be preachers denouncing the society whose sins are being punished. There is, in short nothing terribly strange in regarding natural disasters as warnings or punishments.

Back to Moses and Pharaoh! We are presented with a series of disasters or plagues created not by Moses but by the god who can use nature for his purposes. One might say that holding a people in bondage violates the natural rights of man—all men are created equal—and that nature will go through convulsions in order to right itself. Egypt is visited by a series of plagues or disasters. Moses, the prophetic spokesman of the Hebrews, interprets them as punishment for not freeing the slaves. "Let my people go!" Or else . . . "I told you so . . . do you want more?"

Pharaoh is, of course, a bit of a skeptic. Ah, yes, I can hear him saying, It's a bad year for frogs. A bad year for flies. A bad year for sediment . . . . "Your Majesty, this man Moses says this is happening to punish us for not letting his people go . . ." "He does, does he? And you believe him?" "Well, not exactly. But you know how people are. Even some of the court are beginning to wonder if it might not be a good idea to try some negotiation . . ." But Pharaoh is a hard-liner—God hardens his heart. And he makes the usual discovery of the ultimate loneliness of the hard-liner. He even tries some half-hearted negotiation, but Moses is not interested in compromise. So Pharaoh does not yield, or if he seems to, under great pressure, he repudiates his agreement when the pressure abates.

The conflict runs its grim course. Disaster, denunciation, vacillation. There are hints that many Egyptians, high and low, are beginning to find the slogan "Let my people go" a not unreasonable suggestion. If life runs everywhere true to form we would not be surprised to see the slogan printed somehow on Egyptian cotton shirts sported defiantly on the chests of the heirs of the ruling culture or ruling class to the consternation of Pharaoh and the old guard. After all, Moses himself in his younger days, as a member of the Egyptian elite, was moved to kill in defense of the slaves. The heirs of the oppressors are not born oppressors, and how better can one declare independence from one's father than by showing sympathy for his victims? We know well that the alienation of the heir is the bane of any system of hereditary privilege, the death of "inheritance" itself, the frustration of parental hopes.

The tenth plague seems quite different from the others. An epidemic that swept away Egyptian children? Something more subtly affecting a generation of heirs, for which the actual death of the first-born stands as a puzzling symbol? Whatever it was, it was the last straw. Pharaoh does not mutter "a bad year for first-borns" and dig his heels in. Go, he says, go now, all of you, and take all your things with you. Go, get out, now! Moses has his people ready for this moment. They leave— flee, rather—laden with gifts or spoils or severance compensation to speed them on their way. Pharoah has finally bowed to the demand to "Let my people go."

I am intrigued by the useful ambiguity of "Let my people go." In the present case it means "let us leave, let us depart, allow us to go away . . ." It fits many situations from Israel in ancient Egypt to contemporary ones in which there are border-guards not to keep outsiders out but to keep those on the inside in. Unchain us, free us, let us go . . . . But the phrase also has another sense. Let go of us, free us from your control, your dominance. It may mean "Go away and leave us alone!" as in the demand to "Quit India." Not "allow us to leave" but "Why don't you just go away." And sometimes it may mean "loosen your grip, give up your domination, grant us or recognize our political equality" without the implication that bags necessarily need be packed. "Let my people go!" Let us go away, leave us alone, loosen you grip . . . . There are as many modes of liberation as there are modes of domination. But they may have enough in common so that the sketch of any one will serve as a rough portrait of the family. In any case, "let my people go" has echoed down the ages demanding many forms of liberation from many forms of domination.

The tenth plague is followed by expulsion, release, or flight. The Egyptian bonds are broken and henceforth, for a time, if the Israelites want chains they will have to make them for themselves. The transition between the two phases of the movement from bondage to freedom—liberation is only a step on the way to freedom—is marked by an extraordinary episode. Pharaoh, seeing starkly what life without slaves would mean for Egypt, goes in pursuit of the Israelites. Egyptian high-technology bogs down in the footsteps of desperate refugees; the pursuing army is drowned. The Israelites move beyond the range of Egyptian power. That chapter is ended.

It is to be noted that during the brief period between the Israelite awareness of the Egyptian pursuit and the destruction of the army two remarks—the voice of the people—are thought worth preserving by the muse of history. One is, I think, the first Jewish joke (if not exactly "joke," it is at least bitter wit) on record. "Moses, were there no graves in Egypt that you brought us into the wilderness to die?" The second, echoing endlessly through the ages—"Why did you bring us here? We would rather be slaves in Egypt than die in the wilderness." Better something or other, better fed than dead! But now, for the moment, they are safe. Egypt, not forgotten, still to be longed for, lies behind them. The long march has begun. They carry the bones of Joseph before them, to follow him once more into another homeland.

THE STRUGGLE BETWEEN MOSES AND ISRAEL

If the first phase of this story deals largely with the struggle of Moses against Pharaoh on behalf of Israel the second phase is marked by the struggle between Moses and the people he leads—the struggle between a leader with a vision and his followers who are not visionaries, whose significance lies in the fact that they were *there*, not simply in their idealism or aspirations. They are refugees from slavery, with minds and characters shaped by that overwhelming reality. That is not going to change simply because they have lost their chains. The real difficulty in the journey to the promised land is not the journey itself, whatever its perils, but the transformation of character from slavishness to self-mastery. Without this transformation the journey will end as it began, with the re-creation of a world of children and adults, of dependents and masters; it will be Egypt all over again, with only the names changed. The guide for this journey will reveal the leader as teacher and, as is usually the case, the teacher will have much to learn.

The story of the wandering in the wilderness before the claiming of Caanan lies embedded in the consciousness of the West. I will not trace the steps in faithful order or detail, but I will take note of various conditions, problems, or crises—some major, some minor—that marked the Israelite journey (the basic Mosaic curriculum) and that may need to be faced by any people after the day of liberation.

There is, to begin with, an unexpected lengthening of the transitional period, of what, if we think of it at all, we think of as an interim phase separating our Egypts from our Canaans. Why the delay in moving from the condition of bondage to the state of freedom? The revolution was years ago! Why are we still stalled here? In the case of the Israelites, hardly a survivor from Egypt entered the promised land. A whole generation spent itself in the wilderness wandering between two worlds. Why the delay?

There can be many reasons. We may travel the wrong path and may need to painfully retrace our steps. We may encounter external obstacles that only time can erode. But the main reason, as I have already suggested, is the matter of mind and character. No way of life can be achieved or sustained without its appropriate mind and character or not, at least, in the face of an incompatible condition of the spirit. Old habits are harder to break than old chains. They persist, assert and reassert themselves, overcoming new resolves. Slaves from Egypt sat themselves down in the desert and wept for the fleshpots of Egypt, berating their liberator. Moses, in the end, gave up on them—the old slaves shaped in Egypt, the refugees with memories. He waited for the children to grow up, Israelites who would not carry Egypt with them into their new world.

131

So they loitered for forty years in the wilderness while the old folks died and the new breed of desert kids grew up—new men for the new world.

An obvious consequence of the prolonged period of transition is that you cannot just pack a lunch that will tide you over to the new picnic ground. You will run out of unleavened bread long before you get to Jerusalem. You will even run out of what has been reclaimed from the Swiss deposits of deposed pharaohs. Somehow, disordered though the landscape be, you will have to manage to live off the country. It may seem to require miracles, like manna and flocks of unexpected transient quail, but even travelers to the promised land must eat. Moses discovered this early and was reminded of it often. At least we had water then! Manna, manna! Can't we have some meat for a change? Is there a faint suggestion that they had to learn to ration manna, that hoarding was out? At any rate, they did not perish of hunger or thirst. But they did learn to face the basic problems of survival, from which one may be shielded by the artifices of even an oppressive culture. They had to get used, as we would say, to a different life style. "Temporary" may seem infinitely prolonged, the interim interminable.

They needed, of course, to get organized. There came the fateful moment when it became clear that Moses could not do it alone. "Are you just going to sit here all day, surrounded by all these people, trying to settle every argument?" asked Moses' Midian father-in-law. "Of course," replied Moses, "they want the word of God, through me." "But that's not the way to do it. You'll just wear yourself out with work and wear them out with waiting. What you should do is . . ." And Jethro told him what to do.

So Moses learned to delegate. A necessary, but a fateful step. He looked for, and presumably found, god-fearing, honest and incorruptible men and made them officials who could handle the easy problems and still bring the tough ones to him. Let there be government!

It was, as I said, necessary to get organized, and therefore necessary to find men who could do the work—intelligent, disciplined, loyal. The distinction between the guardians and the people or the flock emerges quite early in the story. We are all, no doubt, consumers, but we are not all responsibility-bearers—trustworthy, diligent—who will, in due course, constitute the priesthoods, the cadres, the parties, the officers of the world. For good, and for ill. I will not trace this familiar story here; but it begins early in the wilderness. Moses, in Midian, is now the head of government and, incidently, party leader.

But the significance of Midian is dwarfed by the overwhelming importance of Mt. Sinai. Moses returns, now as leader, to the scene of his original inspiration to celebrate there the transformation of a mass of freed slaves into a people with its special identity. I note three constitutive elements of the transformation: the covenant, the "constitution," and the law.

The covenant is simply (if we dare say "simply") a solemn or formal agreement creating or acknowledging a structure of obligations. Sometimes a covenant is seen as creating a new political entity, transforming individuals into members, forming a new union, a new state. The idea of a covenant is not being invented by Moses at Sinai; it is not explained; it is understood. It must, in one form or other, be among the most fundamental of social ideas. We solemnly agree to something and all sorts of things are supposed to follow. And, if we have not agreed to something, some things may not exist—like legitimate authority. So a covenant is a special sort of agreement. The Sinai covenant is presented as an agreement—mediated by Moses—between Jehovah and the assembled children of Israel. He becomes their god; they become his people.

Second, what I have called, misleadingly perhaps, the constitution. I refer, of course to the Decalogue, the Ten Commandments. They are part of the Law, but seem somehow more "fundamental"—as Americans might regard the Bill of Rights. Are they "moral" laws as against merely "legal"? Or simply more important? Or a condensed guide to conduct if you don't want to lug the statute books around with you?

Among laws, seen as commandments, the Ten Commandments seem to have a special status as "fundamental."

And third, a great deal of law is formulated or codified or handed down at Sinai—about worship, about property, about injury, about the concerns of daily life.

What is significant is the image of a fateful meeting, a great convention, a founding occasion that somehow serves as the source of the commitment, the morality, the law that shapes a particular polity or community. Sinai is overwhelmingly to the Jews what Philadelphia is marginally to the Americans. (No! I will not stop to argue!)

But even as Moses is struggling with the task of carving the tablets of the new order he is confronted by one of the great crises that haunt the leader dedicated to an ideal. It is the fateful crisis of the golden calf. It is the revolt, always threatening, of those who, having struggled a bit, want it *now*. Having thrown off a set of chains they think that freedom should be enjoyed. They do not want a life of endless discipline, of working for something always beyond the horizon. It may not be quite fair to call it the "hedonic" crisis, but it has something to do with preferring pleasure over sacrifice, or immediate pleasure over continuing sacrifice. Consumer goods now rather than more capital accumulation. Living now, as against the endless postponement of consummation.

It was this revolt, acquiesced in by his chief aide Aaron, that Moses found in process when he came down from the heights. He invoked the loyalty of the old party and conducted a bloody purge—a small civil war. The golden calf was destroyed, its temptations thrust aside, the chastened people resuming its plodding way through the wilderness. Not yet, not yet. *This* is not the promised land. Later! It will be better for our children . . . .

Beside what may be considered the "popular" revolt of the golden calf let us place another serious revolt, the revolt of Korah. This was a challenge to the essential monopoly of power claimed or exercised by Moses, his exclusive access to God. Korah and his fellows were, it seems clear, men of substance, pillars of society, the powerful, the wealthy, the aristocrats—so far as these terms can apply to that situation. They did not see why Moses should alone enjoy the claim to inspired insight, the claim to know God's will. Who was he to set himself so above them, to refuse to share power? Looking for analogies I think of the revolt of Korah as the Whig revolt that failed—a revolt of the aristocrats, the powerful, the rich, against the unshared authority of the king. In England, they won and wrote the history in which their victory is described as a victory for, if not of, the people, instead of a victory of the "interests" against the central executive and the populace. But in the desert, they did not win. There was no compromise, no accommodation. Moses destroyed them and continued his unshared supremacy.

It would be nice to be able to think that the children of Israel, disciplined by hardship, ennobled by their covenant and commandments, advanced, finally, toward their promised land glowing with a special virtue. But the story comes to us full of forebodings and dire predictions. We are led to expect that even in the promised land they will turn away from God and from his commandments and will have to suffer the consequences. So this is a story without a happy ending. There is something ominous about the fact that of the generation to which Moses turns over the leadership two are singled out— Caleb and Joshua. The first is a spy; the second is a general. Specialists in stealth and force. The promised land is not a peaceful haven; it is a new battlefield, a place to be conquered.

And Moses does not go with them. He does not enter the promised land. Why? He is said to have been a hundred and twenty years old when he died, but "his sight was not dimmed nor had his vigor failed." He did not die of exhaustion on the trail. He was allowed a glimpse, but his god did not permit him to enter. So it did not just happen that Moses did not get to the promised land; there is some point to it. But what is the point?

Was it a punishment? Tradition, with some textual support, holds that it is, that Moses became impatient, lost his temper, struck a rock in anger to produce water when he should have followed God's instructions and simply spoken to the rock.

For this god is reported to have said ". . . you shall not lead this assembly into the land which I promised to give them." Let us assume both Moses' act and God's judgment. Even so, it does not seem clear that Moses is being punished. He is being granted a long-due retirement. He is almost being rewarded.

"Ah, Moses," we might hear if we could share God's musing, "Moses, my faithful servant. I see I have tried you too hard. You have done everything I have asked of you. You left your happy life in Midian and returned to Egypt to face fearful odds armed only with your faith in me. You brought the children of Israel out of Egypt. For forty years you have shepherded that unruly flock through the wilderness. They have given you no peace, only torment. You have had to teach them and found them ungrateful. You brought them the law and found them adamant and rebellious. You have had to subdue them, purge them, bring death to many. Few love you. Many fear your hand and your rod. And now I see that you have lost your temper. Or rather, that they have, finally, ruined your temper, made you intemperate. You have survived the Egyptian chapter and the wilderness chapter but you have become hard and brittle and impatient. Where words once served you now use blows. You have earned a rest. I have used you up. I will not make you lead them any more. I will take you to the top of the mountain and show you the land I have promised. But I will spare you the promised land."

Moses, of course, does not argue. Sometime earlier, in a trough of despair after the crisis of the golden calf, he had made a request. All his life he had tried to act for the weak and oppressed, he had tried to lead them from bondage to a better life. He had been immersed in a world of pain and ignorance, of pride and lust, of deceit and war. But through it all he had kept alive a spark of the flame that once burned for him on Sinai, a faint spark of the ideal vision that brought light and warmth to his world. He was not just a politician, not just a warrior, not just a shepherd of men. He was an idealist, a visionary, a seeker of righteousness, a pursuer of truth and virtue, a servant of benign power. One request, after all his striving. Could he see it all? Just once? Could he be shown

136

what it was all about? "Moses," he was told, "you couldn't stand it. It would destroy you."

After that, Moses expected nothing.

•

Even this sketch of the liberation movement led by Moses shows how early the pattern is set in a recognizably modern form. A condition of systematic oppression, a great leader, the ceremonious formulation of a new condition of moral consciousness, miraculous fortune, the discovery or rediscovery of organizational necessity, the struggles for power, the purges, the growing spiritual gap between leader and followers—"the same old story" is found in this very old story.

What strikes me especially is the gap between the leader and the followers. It is not simply that the leader is not one of the people nor can behave, even if he wanted to, as one of the boys. There is a world of difference between having a vision and being oppressed, between seeking the happy oasis and just being thirsty. It is a difference that will inevitably dictate different paths, different directions, even different objectives, different assessments. "OK. So you brought us out of Egypt. And now we have less food, less water, less pleasure, and while they beat us you kill us. Some trip! A better oasis! A promised land! A futile dream!"

So it is almost inevitable that the golden calf will win in the end. It is the popular religion against which the leaders, with strange religions of their own, fight a losing battle. They lead, they preach, they mystify, they perform miracles, and in the end they too fail to reach a promised land. In the process, they stand on one mountain or another and thunder or preach or whisper their sermons or commandments to the awed but uncomprehending multitudes.

The Ten Commandments are instructions about how to behave, based on the awareness of our prevailing faults. You get a fair idea of what we are like by seeing what a moral leader selects for our special attention. The Commandments define the problem; their statement does not solve it. That is why,

I suppose, the central scene in the story, for me, is that moment when the leader comes down from his mountain cradling his carefully carved code only to find that, while he was communing and brooding on high, the people have been melting down their earrings, making their own personal sacrifice, in order to give shape to their idol. It was a bitter moment for Moses. The rest was anti-climax.

Remembering Alexander Meiklejohn

I was not one of the Experimental College boys. It had shut down before I arrived at the University of Wisconsin, but I had been present, an envious intruder, at the 25th reunion in 1957. I was there as one of the later generation of Meiklejohn students, crashing the party to be in on the tribute. And now, another 25 years later, there was to be a reunion without him; a gathering of remnants, a few surviving faculty and perhaps a hundred Ex-college students, all well aged, assembled now not in the presence but in the memory of Alexander Meiklejohn. Veterans of an educational war, the thinning ranks of those who remember Alec. Beyond them, scattered, the even thinner ranks of those who were there, who could remember when, as president, Meiklejohn had stirred, scandalized, divided Amherst.

I did not meet Meiklejohn until all that was over, until he had turned from the struggle to reshape institutions, had retired in some sort of defeat from administrative responsibility, had become famous for his unbowed gallantry in that great lost cause—educational reform. I met him first when he returned to the university to teach for a few years as a member of the philosophy department before retiring from academic life.

The students' lack of institutional memory always seems to surprise the old faculty hand, but to the new student what happened the year before he arrived is merely a little known part of ancient history. So, although the Experimental College had run from 1927 to 1932 and I arrived in 1933, I had never heard of it. I had not heard of Meiklejohn either. "Meiklejohn is back!" I remember the word spreading among the older students on the fringes of whose circle I drifted. There was respect, almost awe, in voices usually stridently iconoclastic. So I signed up for an introductory philosophy course he was to teach, sensing that he was a hero, but knowing very little about it. I am struck by how little was conveyed by what gossip there was about the Ex College. It was different, some sort of educational Eden, briefly flourishing before being done in for reasons or villainies I was too innocent to grasp.

He stepped briskly, smiling, into the classroom—lean, eager, complete. That is, he looked then very much as he looked to me for the next quarter of a century. He seemed old then, and he never seemed to age much after that; old but not feeble, evoking all the comments we make when the old don't act their age. He was lively, cheerful, witty, concentrated, crisp. He was also, although open and friendly, very polite and, I thought, very formal. He brought with him an air of anticipation and excitement.

We were to see Meiklejohn in the classroom, in the conventional academic setting, teaching a course offered by a department. I was not aware of the ironies of the situation. He had been, as we know, an educator—Dean of Brown, President of Amherst, Director of the Experimental College— concerned to create an environment in which teaching and learning would flourish. It is not too much to say that the discrete course, the self-contained class in a subject, the educational institution seen as a loose collection of courses, was the triumphant enemy against which he had always fought. And here he was, at the end of his academic career, enjoying, or condemned to, the transient hospitality of the enemy camp.

He had, on equal terms, the freedom of that city. There was a truce. He was not to disturb the university's peace; he was to teach some course in philosophy—whatever he chose, no doubt—and then, in a few years, he was to retire. I do not think he could have believed very strongly in the significance of what he was doing. But if this is true—as I am now sure that it must have been—we students had no inkling of it. He did not reminisce about the good old days. I do not remember his criticizing the educational system; he did not continue the controversy. He simply taught his courses with zest.

It was a lively class. The mode was discussion of what we were asked to read. He did not explain anything. He smiled a lot, nodded encouragement, listened intently, enjoying it all, welcoming independence, challenging, seldom if ever allowing himself to stand before us as having an idea he was anxious to give us. His enjoyment was contagious and I remember coming into class sullen about the current shape of the universe, warming reluctantly to the discussion, almost cheerful as, at the end of the hour, we streamed down the hill in his lively wake, unwilling to let the argument end.

What was it all about? Why did it mean so much to me? Why, especially since I did not really believe what I thought he meant to say, do I think of it as the turning point of my life?

Wisconsin in the thirties was a progressive, politically alert state proud of its LaFollette traditon. The university was swarming with students from the East who, fleeing or exiled from the seaboard, seem to land either at Chicago or Madison. Madison in the thirties was, with due allowance, something like Berkeley in the sixties.

These were the early Roosevelt days, and the country was floundering in deep depression. In Europe, Hitler loomed in menace. Nevertheless, the university continued in session. The farmers were still there in the Ag School, scientists (did we know any?) were still in their labs—unperturbed worlds, alien worlds. Most of my older friends were in, or trying to get into, medical school or law school. Not for me. I was repelled by the organic intimacy of the one and frightened by the close-argued, heavy-tomed intricacy of the other. What else was

141

there? Some were edging into the chaotic world of government and economics, but I never seemed to understand what they were doing when they did "research" (I still don't). John Gaus was making public administration exciting to a generation of solid young men. I did not feel solid. And there was the Department of Economics. A center of intellectual energy, it was home to something called Institutional Economics. Its great figure, John R. Commons, still lived, faded, on the edge of the campus, and homage was paid to Thorstein Veblen. Younger economists wore the halo of commuters to Washington. But for me, as for many, the dominant force in the university was Selig Perlman.

Perlman to those who encountered him in those days was an unforgettable figure. Swarthy, a nose that was a caricature of itself, a high-pitched squeaky voice, an agonizing stutter, a heavy accent enchancing the impeccable English that painfully emerged, his eyes always fixed on an invisible spot on the ceiling as he excitedly roamed the aisles, he fought adamantly against the popular Marxism of the day, fought it on its own ground with devastating effectiveness.

I was a cradle socialist, fairly familiar with Marx, not a bolshevik, virtually represented, I suppose, by Norman Thomas. Perlman was the first adult I met who knew all about it and, incredibly, did not believe in it. I sat in his classes stunned, fascinated, destroyed, robbed bit by bit of my faith, all certainties dissolved, all direction lost. This is not an attempt to recreate the intellectual ferment of the thirties in a vigorous university. I mention Perlman, as I could mention others, to indicate that Meiklejohn did not appear as a solitary candle in a dim world, a lone mind in a world of clods. The scene was one of vigorous controversy about urgent issues, of powerful assertive teaching. And Meiklejohn, beaten in battle, stripped of his Experimental College, strode into an expectant classroom not quite in the center of things.

What he offered us was the figure of Socrates. That is an interesting selection from among the possible offerings to the young facing a time of troubles. What thirst could Socrates slake? Of course the man sentenced to death by the Athenians on the charge of subversion, of misleading the young, must be with us on the side of the angels. That he refused the invitation to escape the death penalty out of respect for the law that had so unfairly condemned him, out of commitment to the city, was a troubling complication. We were being introduced to the loyal questioner when it seemed obvious that questioning was called for and loyalty was suspect—a fault not a virtue. No, Socrates was not an unflawed hero. He did go, with dignity, into that dark night. But his reasons!

Nor was it easy to accept the Socratic profession of ignorance. It takes time to realize that life is lived in a deep fog lit fitfully by the glitter of illusions, and we thought that he must have known what he denied that he knew, and found his denial affected, insincere.

And even the questioning! How many generations of students have thought that Thrasymachus, the unabashed realist, is merely tricked into silence, outwitted but not fairly refuted. And poor Euthyphro, rushing off, in an early civil-rights case, to report his father for mistreating a slave, waylaid by Socrates and drawn into a diversionary argument about whether the gods love what is right because it is right or whether their loving something makes it right—about whether, as we might put it, public opinion is the measure of rightness. When the injustice is so obvious why must we be stopped to question? There is a kind if impatience with Socrates; in a mood of practical urgency we brush aside the Socratic web and rush into the pit, muttering at Socrates for trying to delay us. Question, yes—but what about action!

So, Meiklejohn brought Socrates to class and introduced him to us. Avoid the unexamined life! Matthew Arnold, offering culture in a Socratic mood to his busy world, wryly reports the criticism: "Death, sin, cruelty stalk among us, filling their maws with innocence and youth, and me in the midst of the general tribulation, handing out my pouncet-box." Well, I have come to love Socrates, but it may not have been love at first sight.

Meiklejohn also brought us, newly published, his book, *What Does America Mean.* To reread it after almost half a century is a bittersweet experience. Ideas long appropriated appear like forgotten old friends, evoking a flood of sharp images, the passions, the doubts, the agonies of youth. To remember Alexander Meiklejohn is to re-examine oneself, to painfully recall the ways of self-defeat, to retrace journeys, to feel the mind begin to stir again over questions never answered but somehow put aside.

What Does America Mean, deeply characteristic as it is, has a special quality of intimacy almost unique among his writings. This is due, I think, to its being written for his college students. It is not condescending, but it has that special unguarded quality of working classroom discourse; it is a teacher's working revelation. It has an air of vulnerability, and now, as then, I feel protective about it. I don't think I want everyone to read it; I would recommend it to only a few of my friends. I do not want to hear what Callicles has to say about it, nor the scoffing of Thrasymachus. I shrink from the burden of defending it, although it is all true.

We are spirits as well as bodies; we have obligations and commitments as well as interests and desires; significance is more than satisfaction; excellence is more than happiness. The pervasive human tragedy is the self-defeat in which the higher is confused with, betrayed to, the lower . . . . Every attempt I make to describe the "doctrine" strikes me as a hopeless caricature. It is, I think, the most personally revealing of Meiklejohn's books, the unshaken base from which he, all his life, conducted his sorties against the materialism he detested.

How did we take all this? In a way, I think, that seemed a part of Meiklejohn's special fate. Generally, we loved where he came out, but we could not accept or understand the philosophy that led him there. Spirit? Whatever is, is solid. We were, on the whole, confident materialists. We felt in our bones that interests were real and obligations snares for the unwary, part of a pernicious ideological superstructure. Happiness made sense. Excellence? Quite all right if it contributed to happiness; but preferable even if it did not?

We overlooked his philosophical oddities because he warmed us by his criticism of the society we lived in, of exploitation, by his scornful rejection of the marketplace as the center of life, of selling as a human transaction, of the competitive success that destroys us. He seemed a prophet crying in the marketplace. He thrilled with sympathy for the notion of a people undertaking, together, to plan for justice and for beauty; with scorn for the idea that each should simply seek his own good. He laughed—and it comforted us—at the idea that the business of America was business. Oddly enough, I cannot remember ever really thinking of him as a socialist or, if the thought crossed my mind, taking it seriously as having anything to do with the core of Alexander Meiklejohn. The issue was deeper; he was an idealist.

As I have said, we found the talk about spirit and obligation to be unreal, something to be treated with polite scepticism. (Perhaps I should not speak of "we" so casually. There were some young Meiklejohnians who eagerly adopted the language of "spirit," but I thought, I must confess, that they simply didn't understand anything. Sometimes "we" shrinks to "I".) But there was another point about which we fought with impolite vigor. *What Does America Mean*? The very title was an irritation. What do you mean, *"What Does America Mean"*? A country doesn't mean anything! It is just spread out there, sometimes where it shouldn't be. It has just grown. Individuals have interests and purposes, Americans have them like everyone else. But "America" is a seething mass of individuals, special interests, classes; it has no special purpose of its own, no unifying, transcending common purpose uniting its diverse members. Years later a classmate unmet for decades shouted in greeting across a room, "common purpose," and it all came flooding back—the excited class, Meiklejohn smiling, nodding, not arguing as we raged against political piety and superstition. Common purpose, indeed!

It was a great stumbling block. Individuals and their interests seemed real enough. Radical enlightenment expressed itself in the view that classes were even realer. It did not seem strange to assert that Jones was a member of the working class whether he realized it or not. It was a fact about him. He needed to be brought to see that he had interests he was not aware of,

that he shared a common class destiny, a common purpose—
something given by the situation, not chosen, to which he
could, if morally asleep, be oblivious, but which, if he awoke,
gave his life significance . . . . It is obvious that the movement
from individual to class consciousness has something in
common with a movement from individual to community
consciousness. But the awareness of class conflict, of class war,
made it difficult to assume a unity that transcended the class
struggle. Classes seemed real; the broader "community" did
not.

I should say, rather, that the broader community seemed real
enough to Meiklejohn but not to some of his devoted followers.
And it made him an easy target. Who, after all was talking about
the political community, the state, those days? Not the phalanx
of left intellectuals: not the individualistic liberal. Fascists?
Simple-minded patriots? Oblivious of his bedfellows,
Alexander Meiklejohn? Obligations, duty, the general will—
clearly the language of the enemy. And we could not cure our
Master of his habit of using that language. We had to try to
defend him. He seemed to be attracted to dangerous ideas.

Looking back, it seems to me that I was not converted to
anything by *What Does America Mean*. When I remember being
shaken it is by Perlman and his persistent argument. To lose
one's socialist faith is one thing; to embrace idealism was quite
another matter, and I was not prepared to do that. But the
special quality of the situation was that we loved Meiklejohn,
loved the quality of his human sympathy and social perception,
the hard integrity of his mind and wit, but viewed with
suspicion, even embarrassment, the idealistic philosophy he
seemed to believe in. I believed in Meiklejohn, but not in what
Meiklejohn believed in.

So it is odd to reread it after all these years. The philosophy
which seemed to me then to be so unsubstantial now seems
to have the irresistable weight of common sense. The argument
does not seem new; it is somehow heavier, right. But to my
chagrin, the fervor of my accord with the criticism of the
market place and all that seems to have abated a bit. How can
the student, the disciple of Alexander Meiklejohn, explain the

depressing drift into the reasonableness of the editorial page of the *Wall Street Journal*? The god that failed, to be sure, but is that really enough? And why, unlike years ago, when I read "We must take the social order in our hands and set it right," do I shy like a frightened horse or shudder like Burke presented with an interesting new proposal? I will, of course postpone any attempt to answer these depressingly interesting questions . . . .

So there was the figure of Socrates, and there was *What Does America Mean*. There was also a faint expectation of philosophical conflict in the air. Max Carl Otto was a popular figure in the university—an exponent of a variety of pragmatism, a follower of James and Dewey. Since Meiklejohn was an idealist the stage was set for a Wisconsin variation on Harvard's earlier James-Royce encounter. It did not quite come off. I had always liked William James and had, therefore tried to study Dewey and was disposed to be a pragmatist. I was also prepared to like Otto, who was iconoclastic about the gods and derisive about Kant and that sort of thing. But Otto tended, I thought, to ridicule what he disagreed with and was quite unfair in his characterization of Meiklejohn. At any rate, there was no great feast of argument between them. Still, I tried to show Meiklejohn that he and Dewey really agreed about everything. He smiled and shook his head; I didn't convince him.

In my last year at the University of Wisconsin, I was still at loose ends, and Meiklejohn suggested that I take up graduate work in philosophy. That, he said, meant either Harvard or Berkeley. Since his home was now in Berkeley, I did not consider Harvard and one fall day in 1937 I trudged up the hill to the house, about a half-mile from the Berkeley campus, that was to be Meiklejohn's home for the next quarter of a century.

I was rescued from the miseries of life as a graduate student in philosophy by World War II, but not before I had endured some four years of it, living most of the time within a few blocks of the Meiklejohn home on La Loma. His chief activity during that period was in connection with the San Francisco

School of Social Studies, which he founded and struggled to maintain. It was a venture in adult education, something very close to Meiklejohn's heart. I was drawn in to the edge of the work of the school, asked to teach several classes. There was a lively faculty group. Meiklejohn took a hand, Helen (Mrs. Meiklejohn) was enthusiastically engaged, John Powell from the Experimental College faculty acted as director (was director I should say, but John never seemed quite like a director to me), and there was the sparkling team of Hogan and Cohen. And several others I never got to know very well. John Powell has written interesting accounts of the school. I did not witness the throes of its creation, nor was I there when, during the war, it closed its doors.

It was an attempt to create an institution within which a persistent effort to develop the political and social understanding necessary for the life of a democratic citizen could be sustained. It was not concerned with credit towards a degree, nor with vocational retooling or promotion nor even with cultivating the enjoyment of leisure. It was to be a place for adults to study their common concerns as members of the polis. "School," I suppose, is the inevitable name, although it is a name laden with doom. But we seem to have no better name for what, in any case, we hardly have at all. Still, there is a not unreasonable dream that adult members of a democratic community will, as a normal part of their lives, read and gather to discuss materials out of which a common understanding will grow, a school that need never come to an end, a habit from which there is no graduation, a community made by taking thought together . . . Amherst, Wisconsin, San Francisco—a story with the same golden thread. Not, this time, on a green New England college campus, not in an enclave by the shore of a lake on a middle-western university campus, but in a part of an office building in downtown San Francisco or in the rooms of a Santa Rosa Junior College in their deserted evenings.

My memory of those days, little as I trust it, is of a Meiklejohn slightly withdrawn from the battle. He was in it, and his presence was clearly indispensible, but he was more like Moses raising his arms over the battlefield than like the commander in the field. A bit remote; a good part of his mind otherwise occupied. That, at least, is my impression; although I'm sure it understates the degree of his devotion to the school, to adult education.

He was also engaged with the American Civil Liberties Union. I had not yet awakened to the delights of constitutional law and I wondered why he was so interested in something as unimportant as civil liberties. The Northern California branch was in a running dispute with the national office about the inclusion of Communists on the ACLU board—something like that. Meiklejohn, of course, argued against the exclusion of Communists—as he was also to argue brilliantly against the exclusion of Communists from university faculties. But apart from this particular controversy, his concern with civil liberties and with the ACLU was deep and persistent. And it had that odd quality I have already mentioned. Civil libertarians hailed him as their champion; few have matched his enlightened passion about the First Amendment, his defense of freedom of speech. But, of course, while they loved where he came out they did not, generally, understand or agree with how he got there. Most thought of civil liberties as belonging to individuals "against" the state. Meiklejohn thought of them as the powers of citizens implied by their public function (a point I hope to make clearer when I speak of *Free Speech*). Puzzled by his reasons, enthusiastic about his conclusions. Even, perhaps, forgiven his reasons for the sake of his conclusions . . . .

Eventually, there were consequences. Meiklejohn always insisted on the crucial distinction between the powers or civil liberties of the citizen as ruler and the civil rights of the citizen as subject. He considered the ACLU as primarily dedicated to the former, to the protection of the integrity of the mind of the sovereign people. In the end, if I may pass lightly over intervening years, he became increasingly unhappy with the tendency of the ACLU to move away from his conception of its proper role. Finally, he withdrew from the ACLU. He withdrew quietly. He did not, he told me, want to resign with a public statement of disagreement. But, with disappointment and regret, he left the organization he had cared for for so many

149

years. In the sixties I had actually joined the ACLU and was, for a time, on the board of the Berkeley branch. I left in a huff, in disgust, over what I thought was the ACLU's utter failure to understand academic freedom and its stupid tolerance of disorder on the campus. I felt quite Meiklejohnian, but I must stop short of tarring him by association.

So, in those pre-war years Meiklejohn was busy with the San Francisco School of Social Studies, with the ACLU, and with what seemed to me to be a booming social life. He and Helen had many friends on the faculty and in the area, and visitors from the East were always dropping in. Lunches, teas, dinners, social evenings seemed to besiege the carefully protected mornings in the study. The study in which, at that time, he was writing *Education Between Two Worlds.*

Education Between Two Worlds is a sustained, impassioned attack on the competitive individualism which he calls "protestant capitalism," or when he warms up, "Anglo-saxon protestant capitalism." Not exactly, for Meiklejohn, a newly discovered villain. In fact, from start to finish, grappling with life as a teacher, what seems to unmask itself everywhere as the enemy is, on the one hand, the adamant assertion of the private or "selfish" interest—however enlightened the self—as the proper aim of all action, and the companion view that on the intellectual plane the mind was to rest content with "the way it seems to me" as the final view of things, polished with the politeness of a tolerance for the regrettably different views of other minds. We each have desires; we each have opinions; and if we have good manners we can live with the unavoidable conflicts without the futile struggle to impose a common "good" on the teeming world of desire, or a common "truth" on the mad and blind world of opinion. Some such view, encountered everywhere, was, to Meiklejohn, the denial of the possibility of human fellowship and human sanity, a rejection of Jesus and Socrates.

The book has a dramatic form. Something has broken down and we need to rebuild, but we stand baffled amidst the rubble. Surprising studies of key figures trace the story: Comenius, the frustrated hero of the old religious order; Locke, the destructive compromiser; Matthew Arnold, the yearning victim; Rousseau, the incoherent prophet of a new order. The individual studies are gems in themselves, fresh, perceptive, controversial interpretations; made, as they are put together, to carry the story line. The story is really simple, stark, central. The old religious order with God, and the conception of men as his children, a human family under a single moral law—that conception of the world is shattered, gone, not really believed in. And even when not explicitly renounced, we have learned to put religion to one side, to separate it from the prudential world, banish it to a private realm. And, generally, the church has been replaced by the state as the central public institution. The public school, under the aegis of the state, has become our chief teacher. Can it, how can it, what can it, teach? The intellectual basis of the old order is gone; we are left with the competitive individualism of an essentially warring world, fundamentally inadequate; we seem not to have developed the understanding that would do for the state what religion had done for the church . . . . We are, as Arnold mourned, between two worlds—one dead, the other powerless to be born . . . .

I must pause over the relation of Meiklejohn to religion. It must have seemed to me that anyone who was "idealistic," who spoke of duty and obligation, of brotherhood, of unity, was religious. Meiklejohn even looked a bit clerical; he had bishops and rabbis among his friends; he spoke lovingly of the culture of Burns and the Bible; he wrote tenderly of Comenius. And yet . . . he was not a churchgoer, he was not pious, he was not devout. He did not believe the religious story in the terms in which it was told, and he did not pretend he did, or act as if he did, or ever use a religious prop to support an argument, or ever wrap anything in religious mystery. Risking all sorts of misunderstanding I will assert that in all the years I knew him he was absolutely unreligious. Unreligious. "Atheist" does not describe it, since what we usually think of as atheism is merely a form of fundamentalism; and to deny the literal truth of a parable is as misguided as to affirm it. His position, made explicit in *Education Between Two Worlds*, is that some deep intuitions were once expressed in religious form and language, but the religious form now no longer serves them; that these still-valid insights need to find adequate expression—"political" (in a proper sense) rather than religious.

The difficulty with this analysis is that it is both undeniable and unpalatable. Religion *has* become for us an essentially private matter; church and state have become "separate"; and the state, moving into the space left by the shrinking church, has become the instrument through which we seek the public good. Through which, especially, we seek to educate. At the same time, we can hardly be said to have a view of the "state" which would lead us to trust it with the care and nurture of the soul. We would need to think better of the state. But that "thinking better of the state" seemed almost to be the distinctive mark of the enemy—of the authoritarians or totalitarians against whose exaltation of the state we were being driven to a defiant affirmation of "individualism." Meiklejohn seemed all too willing to think sympathetically about the state, about government which, more deeply understood, might be made a worthy servant of the community's aspirations. But he was swimming against the tide. The liberal mind found "pluralism" more safely congenial; conservatives, when not drifting into a libertarian folly, wanted, at least, to shrink the public sector. Government, however much we depended upon it, was in disrepute; education, therefore, in serious disarray.

I read parts of *Education Between Two Worlds* in manuscript, but I was not able, at that time, to get a sense of the work as a whole. I agreed with the formulation of the problem. A long section in which Meiklejohn dealt with Dewey seemed to me to be right, but to be too polemical and somehow not very satisfactory. I found it hard to disagree with what Meiklejohn offered as the way out, but I also felt unmoved by it, and a bit let down. I suppose I expected, as a friend of mine said, that he would pull a rabbit out of the hat, and I didn't see a rabbit—although I don't suppose I would have recognized one if it had been—as perhaps it was—produced. But I was a bit preoccupied with exams and the approaching war. I was an isolationist in those days, reluctant, as we were saying, to pull the chestnuts of the British Empire out of the fire, horrified by Hitler, appalled by the power of the Axis, raised on the futility of war, the injustice of Versailles—a stranger to the culture of guns. Meiklejohn was not an isolationist, but I cannot remember arguing with him. When, some months before Pearl Harbor, I was drafted, Meiklejohn said only, "You will not want to miss the formative experience of your generation." I was startled by the unexpected remark, but it seemed to make sense; and in any case, Pearl Harbor overrode doubts.

Sometime in 1942, just out of OCS, I had a few days in the New York area and went to Annapolis for a day to visit Meiklejohn who was spending some time as a friendly observer at St. John's College. It was the only glimpse I had of him on a small, eastern college campus, and I don't think I ever saw him happier and more at home. It was also the first glimpse I ever had of that lovely world. Meiklejohn belonged there, as, I suppose, he did not belong in Madison, as he did not belong in San Francisco, as he really did not belong in Berkeley. When the roll is called, it will be Meiklejohn of Amherst. It was that day, I think, that he told me of his visit to Woodrow Wilson, still in the White House. "Ah Meiklejohn" sitting up in his sickbed the Scot president of Princeton greeted the Scot president of Amherst, "When I get out of here we must start a college together!"

That day at St. John's remains in memory. Green, quiet, sunny. Meiklejohn smiling, loitering at the tennis courts, alert at the back of a classroom, jesting with Scott Buchanan about something Scott was brooding over. A Meiklejohn absorbed, springy-stepped, happy, in a world he knew to the core and loved.

After the war I returned to Berkeley and soon settled into teaching at the university. Meiklejohn was there on La Loma. The San Francisco School of Social Studies was gone. *Education Between Two Worlds* had been quietly received by the world. And Meiklejohn was launching his career as expounder of the meaning of the First Amendment. Berkeley had lost its bucolic air and seemed quite in the center of things. We were excited about big issues—the United Nations, the bomb, hopes for peace and a new order, growing tensions with Russia as the cold war developed, Senator McCarthy and the hunt for subversives . . . . Against this background, the great dramatic episode for the university, and for Meiklejohn, was the faculty loyalty oath fight of 1949-1950.

It was a bitter, hearbreaking fight, and in spite of some ultimate judicial triumph and the vindication and recall of the non-signers, in spite, even, of the amazing persistence of a determined but divided faculty, the feeling I now have as I try to recapture the memories of those days is a deep sense of defeat—a defeat which tormented me even then and from which I have probably never really recovered.

Faculty members were required to sign a statement disavowing membership in (or belief in the principles of) the Communist party, as a condition of continuing employment. There were, of course, all sorts of issues, motives, pressures, questions, variations in formulation, but I think a crude formulation which ignores vanished contextual subtleties will serve best. Should a Communist be allowed to teach in the university?

There was a simple common sense view that Communists did not believe in democracy, would destroy it if they could, and that it made no sense to give them the chance to undermine the democratic educational system. (How do you convince the man in the street that you should hire your enemy to corrupt your children?) At the level of academic, not "man in the street," or the "people out in the state" common sense, the view was that an acknowledged Communist had a disciplined commitment to a dogma as interpreted by the party, expressed as the party-line, and was not, therefore, committed to the free pursuit of truth, did not have the open-mindedness essential to the community of scholars. The regents, in requiring the disclaimer, were standing on popular ground. Nevertheless, the faculty found itself drawn into a bitter prolonged fight.

In a simpler world, one of our respected colleagues would have simply announced, truly, that he was a member of the Party, that he believed its program was best for America, that he wanted to continue his scholarly work and teaching, that he could not take the oath without lying and he wouldn't do

154

that, and that he didn't see why he should be fired. Alas, no one stepped forward to give us a concrete case to fight about. We were not to know, made it a point of honor not to try to find out, if there were real live Communist party members on the faculty. The matter was to be fought out on "principle."

But what principle? Many, if not most, thought that a dedicated Communist was as unfit to teach as a dedicated Fascist, as (a bit *sotto voce*) a dedicated Catholic (the pope, infallibility and all that . . .), as in fact a "dedicated" anything—if the dedication was to anything but the unbiased pursuit of truth. And in any case the faculty in its "practical" mood (an amusing madness that sometimes seizes it) did not think a defense of Communists would sell in the provinces. So that the basic question, involving the difficulties of the relation between commitment and truth or between passion and cognition, was avoided so far as was possible. Instead, we retreated to such things as: party membership involves guilt by association; actions are punishable, not beliefs; oaths are silly and don't work because liars take them routinely; singling out a group like professors was discriminatory and insulting; the regents had no business meddling with hiring and firing which were governed by faculty procedures; "academic freedom" was being violated; and so on. Early in the struggle, tragically, I thought, the faculty—the Academic Senate—abandoning the heartland, formally endorsed the regent's anti-Communist policy—while the fight continued on a variety of the other grounds.

Meiklejohn had published the clearest defense of the position of the Communist teacher and scholar in the university world. If the person was otherwise qualified, the fact that he believed in communism and joined the party was an exercise of judgement and a matter of intellectual freedom—not a ground for disqualification. Beyond the question of "rights," he also argued the educational advisability of having convinced communists in the educational institution. And, of course, he was highly sensitive to the procedural matters that lie at the heart of academic freedom. It was a brilliant argument, and I agreed (and still agree) with it completely.

During the long struggle, Meiklejohn felt himself to be in a delicate position. He cared passionately about the issue and thought it was the most significant crisis of the modern American university. He had close friends on the faculty, yet he was not a member of the university; it was his battle, but he could not take a direct part in it. The leader of the embattled faculty of those who fought against the oath requirement, was Edward Tolman; shy, courageous, sensitive, intelligent, a man of utter integrity. Tolman lived on La Loma also, his home just across the way from Meiklejohn's. They were old friends. Tolman was a scientist, a psychologist, and not a constitutional or political theorist. He did not formulate the issues or elaborate defenses of abstract positions. He acted out of a sense of responsibility for more vulnerable colleagues, out of an instinct for freedom and decency as well as a conviction that there was something improper about the demand for an oath, for a disclaimer of belief. Close as he was to Meiklejohn, I do not think he found his ideas, his theories, congenial. Nor did many who were taking part in the fight. Meiklejohn was, after all, the spokesman for the "absolutist" position, the defender of the right of Communists to teach. That was a position that, as I said, was abandonned by the Academic Senate which, after endorsing the regents anti-Communist policy, could no longer continue the fight on those grounds. But the play ran on, without Hamlet, for a bitter year—the grounds of opposition constantly narrowing as the faculty, involved heavily in negotiation, lost one piece of ground after another.

Meiklejohn, uninvolved in the day to day struggle, not a party to deals and concessions, had no need to change his position or to drop the main issue. He continued to follow the battle closely. I, and others, dropped in frequently to discuss the situation with him. He was especially concerned about the position of the left-wing junior faculty members, not by this time, it must be said, the center of the faculty's general concern. Meiklejohn seldom asked me to do anything, but once, as I was going off to some meeting to plan the next move, he asked me to raise a question about the general indifference to the fate of a young "radical." I intended, because he asked me, to do so. But I found that when the moment came I shrank from doing it. I was being practical that week, and I could not bring myself to do something so quixotic. I still remember the bitter taste of failing to do one of the few things Meiklejohn ever asked me to do.

So, throughout the oath fight Meiklejohn was on the sidelines, never inciting others to fight, sympathetic, clear headed and at times, I think, almost heartsick. Perhaps not heartsick; he was used to being with a losing minority and never seemed to lose his verve. And always, he was surprisingly realistic. Above all, in all the turmoil he never seemed to lose sight of the fundamental issues, never seemed to lose his appreciation of the quality of human action. Had he been on the faculty, I cannot imagine him signing the oath.

More than a decade later, during the student unrest, the so-called free speech movement, Meiklejohn was still on the sidelines, living a bit more quietly on La Loma. He was, of course, deeply interested in what was going on, and many of the student leaders found their way to his home. And I would drop in frequently while he was lingering over the paper at breakfast and bring him up to date with what I thought was going on. (I was moving steadily from young turk to old guard.) He was, by this time the grand old man of free speech. And it was assumed that he would be in sympathy with a movement that unfurled the flag of free speech—a movement of students in a university which was large and impersonal and generally criticized as being indifferent to the educational fate of its undergraduates. Meiklejohn liked students and he listened to them and understood them. But while in the faculty oath fight he had provided active intellectual support for the position opposed to that of the regents, on the "free speech movement" he was, I believe, publicly silent. His position, as I remember it: in so far as students were objecting to a fragmented undergraduate education, he agreed that much of undergraduate education was a shambles. He did not think that students knew how to remedy the situation and did not think that student participation in the running of the institution made any sense. This may perhaps surprise some who misunderstood his deep sympathy for students. But educational matters were, in fact, a very small part of the student revolt in any case.

As for the so called free speech issue—the right of students to pursue their politics on campus—Meiklejohn's position was clear. Students had no "right," not even a First Amendment right, to engage in political activity on campus. "The issue," he once said to me, "should not be put in terms of rights. It is entirely one of educational policy. If in the judgement of the university authorities it is conducive to the educational purposes of the university to permit political activity, then it should permit it; if not, not." I do not think that, as an administrator, he would have compromised on this fundamental point. So, while sympathetic to the students, he did not agree with their position. On the other hand, it would have been very difficult for him to come to the aid of an administration whose exercise of its authority he regarded as an educational disgrace. So, he listened to everyone, nodded, asked gentle questions, did not argue, did not incite, did not make public declarations. In private, he was as close to bitterness as I had ever seen him.

When we think of his first 70 years, it is Meiklejohn the educator. For the two decades after that he is, of course, Meiklejohn of the First Amendment. Even earlier he had been interested in law and the Constitution. I remember being surprised, at Wisconsin, by his defense of the Supreme Court against Roosevelt's attack; a packed auditorium, Meiklejohn cheerfully taking the unpopular side. A single sentence of his floats intact out of memory's haze: "It was a greater mind than Justice Holmes' that said 'Only the Permanent changes!'" Meiklejohn had been close to Walton Hamilton and Malcolm Sharp, two great teachers of the Constitution, and had seen the fertility of the Constitution and law as teaching material. And, of course, there was his long involvement with the ACLU. But it was with the publication of *Free Speech* in 1948 that he emerged as a great interpreter of the First Amendment.

The First Amendment is, as every lawyer knows, a complicated and treacherous swamp—a simple statement overlaid by a thick and perplexing gloss. A modern landmark was the work of Oliver W. Holmes, Jr., who had mitigated the apparently unqualified character of "no law abridging the freedom of speech" by adding, to put it crudely, "except when there is a clear and present danger" of something or other . . . . How clear, how present, how great a danger of what to what are questions that have engaged a great deal of legal ingenuity. The upshot is that there is to be no abridging of the freedom of speech except, of course, to avoid "danger," and history and practice have worked out details. It has been worked out in such a way, moreover, that, on the whole, we do not complain of too little freedom of speech. To take "no law" as actually meaning "no law" is an affront to our practical sense, hopelessly "absolute"; and Holmes and clear and present danger, have set it all right.

Meiklejohn, if I may dare to oversimplify, did two things. He narrowed the scope of the First Amendment by reading "freedom of speech" to mean the freedom of political speech; and, thus narrowed, gave it a preferred position among forms of communication. So that government may not abridge the freedom of political discussion, even on the ground that the government thinks the discussion is dangerous; "non-political" speech—commercial speech, for example—does not enjoy that degree of protection and may be, as are other activities, governed by "due process of law." In short, one kind of speech is given more protection and the other kinds of speech are given less protection.

This interpretation—narrowing and deepening the First Amendment's protection—is supported by a rather surprising move. I remember the day I first heard it. Profesor Jacobus tenBroek and I were sitting in Meiklejohn's study while he read to us an argument against the power of congressional committees to probe the political beliefs of citizens. As the issue had been put, there were said to be three branches of government, each with its necessary powers, and, posed against these, the private individual with his desire to express himself and his desire for privacy—a private desire which must give way to public necessity. But, Meiklejohn pointed out, there are really four branches of government—the fourth branch being the electorate, a branch of government with special functions to perform and with powers that must be protected if that function is to be properly performed. Each citizen is a member of the electorate and in that capacity has the powers of a public office, quite apart from his private interests and rights. The First Amendment, Meiklejohn argued, should be read not as referring to the private right of expression, but as a statement of the powers of the electorate and the assurance that these powers—assembly, speech, publication—are not to be interfered with by another, an inferior, branch of government. The amendment is the fundamental guarantee of the political power of the people, acting as the electorate, a power so fundamental as to be properly taken as, relatively, absolute. To thus relate the meaning of the First Amendment to the theory of self-government through the fourth branch is, I think, a stunning stroke of genius.

Free Speech, reissued with some added papers as *Political Freedom*, is probably the presently most readable of Meiklejohn's books. And it has some characteristic Meiklejohnian features. It is both crisply written and full of passion—as usual; it is also, as usual, immoderate and defiantly iconoclastic; it is an analysis, but it is also an attack. It is an attack on a great popular hero and a related attack on the great popular principle for which the hero is honored as creator—on Justice Holmes and on "clear and present danger."

Holmes is surely one of the most popular of American legal giants, and to attack him is to ask for trouble. But Meiklejohn finds the combination of hard-headed "realism" or cynicism eked out by sheer sentimentality an example of the quality of mind that marks the failure of education. So with some preliminary gestures of respect he launches a powerful attack on the mind of Holmes. But, of course, the worshipers of Holmes will simply set their dented idol back on its feet and continue the idolatry. And, as I have indicated, he rejects the position that the meaning of the First Amendment is adequately expressed by the view that there is a personal right (a natural right?) of free expression limited only by the need to avert a clear and present danger. But his own position involves a rejection of competitive individualism and a troublesome view of the state that seems both innocent and dangerous. Clear and present danger seems good enough to many warriors in the civil liberties struggle. To reject it is impractical, but it is nice to have someone around (like Meiklejohn) to take an "absolutist" position that, dangerous or not, freedom of speech should never be abridged. So, without being understood, Meiklejohn was hailed as the great First Amendment absolutist—stirring, but, as a philosopher, naturally a bit idealistic . . . .

Meiklejohn's central preoccupation during the last decades of his life was with the First Amendment and with the claims upon his time and attention flowing from his stature as the defender of the absolute right of freedom of speech. In this connection I must speak of a month-long session held at the Center for the Study of Democratic Institutions in Santa Barbara. The Center had been established and was presided over by Robert M. Hutchins who, after a brief and stormy time with the Ford Foundation went off to create a serious non-academic intellectual center. A month, one summer, was to be devoted entirely to a consideration of the First Amendment and, in addition to the resident members of the Center, a number of others were invited—Meiklejohn, of course, and Harry Kalven of the University of Chicago Law School, and I, among them.

It was an interesting ramble through some of the thickets in that field of constitutional law. Meiklejohn's ideas had been published, so they were part of the background, familiar to us. We went through a number of papers without unusual enthusiasm. I took up four days with the first presentation I ever made of what, some years later, was to be developed and published as *Government and the Mind*. Kalven, full of wit and knowledge, was, I think, the star of the show. Lots of indecisive meandering, mostly enjoyable. Meiklejohn sat there quiet and attentive, saying very little but, as usual, everyone seemed to be speaking primarily to him, vying to impress him. His ideas, as I said, were familiar and, on this occasion, not being presented as having to be argued for. I remember only a

161

growing sense of regret that the negative form of the First Amendment might obscure the possible responsibility of government for cultivating and enhancing the life of the public mind. But on the whole, the conference left matters about where they had been. What else should one expect?

What was memorable to me about that month with Meiklejohn at Santa Barbara was not the free speech discussion; it was education. Assembled there, almost accidentally, were some of the leading figures in the modern history of American higher education. There was Hutchins of the University of Chicago; there were Scott Buchanan and Stringellow Barr of St. John's; there was Meiklejohn of Amherst and Wisconsin. (The missing voice was Dewey's, perhaps, but Dewey [or his followers in the stronghold of the Teacher's College] had never really hurled himself against the formidable institutional structure of the American college or university.) Hutchins was an impressive figure. He presided with intelligence, grace, courtesy, and beyond presiding, he had a mind of his own. He worked hard, still getting to his desk by five or so every morning, winding up a fair day's work by 10AM. He had lived at the center of conversation and argument for years, had heard everything, read widely, listened patiently, assimilating what came to him to a strong structure of convictions. Striking, courtly, formidable. He was, as I said, trying to create a new kind of intellectual center, beyond the gates of the university. He was devoted to the attempt, but the Center did not, I think, live up to his hopes. Still, it was a gallant attempt and Hutchins seemed relatively untouched by the bitter infighting that swirled around him—small stuff, no doubt, compared with what he had endured in his attempts to launch and protect his college at the University of Chicago. What little I knew of the Chicago enterprise I did not find terribly congenial. I did not like its metaphysical basis, and I had resented Hutchins' articulate visibility. He had, as spokesman for reform in higher education, stood in the place I thought should have been Meiklejohn's. I thought the Experimental College was a better idea than the Chicago plan, that Meiklejohn had a deeper mind than Hutchins', that Hutchins had a better public-relations flair . . . . But all that was long ago. Both shared a common experience of defeat in the educational wars, and the relation between the two of them was warm and friendly. It was a delight to see them at the same long table.

And there was Scott Buchanan. He was one of the permanent members of the Center and, to my mind, one of the most powerful and interesting influences there—learned, broodingly thoughtful, a ranging irreverent imagination, a patient gentle wit. His presence was, I thought, comforting and reassuring to Hutchins. Scott had been an undergraduate at Amherst during Meiklejohn's presidency and Meiklejohn always remembered that when he was "fired" from the presidency, Scott had said to him: "You have been Socrates; now it is time for you to be Plato." Buchanan sketches part of his own intellectual history in the introduction to *Poetry and Mathematics*, but I don't remember him telling the story of St. John's in detail. Meiklejohn was close to St. John's as he was never close to Chicago, although he had reservations about the conception of liberal education as defined by the trivium and the quadrivium. Still, St. John's was the embodiment of a serious conception, and Meiklejohn enjoyed his times in friendly residence there. Buchanan and Barr had left St. John's some time before this meeting in Santa Barbara. Scott mentioned wryly that when he wrote the description of the program in the first catalogue he thought it would be changed every year; he had not expected it to become a bible. Buchanan was close to Meiklejohn and close to Hutchins and, as we sat there, the only one of the three whose institutional efforts still had a concrete expression. The Experimental College was gone; Chicago had dismantled the college after Hutchins had left; but St. John's, abandoned by Buchanan and Barr, had survived, still living, I think, on Scott's inspiration. But they were all retired from the struggle, assembled now to discuss the problems of intellectual freedom under the First Amendment.

In those two post-war decades Meiklejohn lived, as I have said, on the edge of the campus, with many faculty friends but nevertheless at arm's length from the university. He often appeared on campus. Every Friday a group of a dozen or so faculty from different departments met for lunch in a room in the faculty club. Meiklejohn was a member of this group and often on Friday I would walk down the hill with him to the club. It was a relaxed, loud, jesting lunch—the pursuit of truth adjourned for the moment—seldom serious, gossipy, full of confident self-assertion. Meiklejohn sat there, well liked, one of the group, joining in laughter but seldom evoking it, quiet and observant, not in the least interfering with the unabashed display of unharnessed faculty wit. But I would wonder what he thought of it all, coming down from his study in anticipation of intellectual fellowship, a foray into the world that was essentially hostile to all he believed in about college education—hard-headed successful scholars, teachers of disciplines, rugged individualists of the mind, personally very friendly, but professionally hostile to almost everything Meiklejohn as an educator had always stood for, not only hostile toward but triumphant over . . . . Meiklejohn the teacher in the midst of the successful professoriate. It could really only be a luncheon truce although the group, I think, was unaware of how deeply he was at odds with them; they were professors; he was an educational reformer—enemies by nature. Strangely, of all the years of talk I remember only one exchange: "Alec, its amazing that at ninety you can polish off that strawberry ice cream! How do you do it?" "Oh," came the reply, "I've always followed a rule: anything I want, but never a second helping."

I had long been restless about the nature of lower-divison education and when I returned to teach at Berkeley in 1963 I began an effort to establish a version of the Experimental College on the Berkeley campus. The program did not go into operation until 1965 and Meiklejohn was not there to see it, but I had discussed my plan with him before he died. It was, as I said, based on what I understood, or perhaps fantasized, of the Wisconsin experiment; but I was hesitant to discuss it in detail with Meiklejohn or to involve him in it in any way. I felt that there was something presumptuous in my trying to do what he had done, and I did not want to ask his approval or involve him in criticism. But I told him about it and about the progress of the enterprise as it made its way through the obstacle course of committee approval. He listened patiently. He made no suggestions; I don't think he even asked any questions. He was, now that I think of it, utterly unexcited by the prospect. I was, and I knew it, and he knew it, no Alexander Meiklejohn. He could have stopped me with a word, but he did not utter it, so I went ahead stubbornly. At one point he asked, firmly, that I not call it the Experimental College. But by that time there was a budget line for an Experimental Collegiate Program (not a title of my choosing) and the program became known as the Experimental Program—close enough to make me uneasy. It did not occur to me then, but he must have had deep misgivings. It does occur to me now, but I am far from regretting the adventure—part of which I have recounted in *Experiment at Berkeley*. Nothing remains of it at Berkeley, but oddly enough there is a program at the University of Wisconsin that claims lineal descent from the original Experimental College.

Meiklejohn continued the pattern of life he had established until the end. The intensity of his social life abated; his daily walks in the hills were a bit less brisk; he lingered a bit longer over his breakfast coffee, chatting leisurely with me when I dropped in to see him on my way to the campus, less anxious to get to his study to write. He told me one day, a bit upset, that he was having trouble writing—that he seemed to be writing in circles. He allowed me to dissuade him from publishing a short review that I thought was uncharacteristically personal in its polemics. And then, one day, neatly, without fuss, he took a deep breath and died.

How can I describe the special quality of Meiklejohn's presence? Beyond the crisp alertness, the sense that everything was being enjoyed, that every moment was a special occasion, beyond the flashing wit, the friendly invitation to combat, the unpretentious formality, the encouraging smile that seemed to tempt everyone into putting his best foot forward or to live for a while on tiptoe. Most deeply I think it was a matter of awareness, a consciousness of significance, the sense that the world contained more things than one ordinarily supposed.

Meiklejohn seemed to see more. Some of his responses—a smile of appreciation, a quick flare of indignation—came unexpectedly, so that you became aware, at least, that you were missing something. I remember an experience I had in a plane while a movie was being shown on a screen. I watched idly, not wearing the headset for sound. I saw lips moving, arms waving; it was strange and dull. But once in a while those around me burst into laughter, and I realized that I was missing something that was going on before my uncomprehending eyes. They were aware of something that was there that made the situation comic; I was blind, or deaf, to it. Meiklejohn always seemed to be tuned in to a richer world—one in which more things were going on than met the ordinary casual eye. In his contagious presence you became aware of stories, plots, dramas you would not have noticed on your own and which, when you left his presence, seemed to fade out of mind, persisting only like the memory of a dream. As his student, evoking the aid of his memory, I do not find myself asking, "what would Meiklejohn say," but rather, "what am I missing that Meiklejohn would *see*?"

As for "what would Meiklejohn say?" I must say something about how he said things. In a classroom, or in the midst of a group engaged in discussion, he said, in fact, very little. It is not that he would not take part in the exchange; but what he said always had the quality of an intervention. A question, a quick short sentence. I cannot remember him making anything like a sustained argument, or pressing a point, or loosing a barrage of words. His interventions were often startling and would send the discussion off on a fresh tack or recall it from a diversion; but they were brief, friendly, good humored, often witty. The unit of discourse was, for him, the single short sentence set off by an encouraging nod, a smile, or even a defiant thrust of the chin.

But his speeches were quite another matter. I heard him speak in public many times, but I do not remember him ever speaking extemporaneously. He read what he had to say; it was prepared in advance. He read well, as such things went, but he did not make it up as he went along. And it was quite a different

Meiklejohn. I was often shocked by it; it did not seem in character. Or rather it was, since he spoke often enough, another side of his character. He was nervous beforehand and he began calmly enough, but soon his voice rang out, he almost shouted—sometimes did—and there was very little diffidence at the heart of the argument. Full of fervor, full even of denunciation, hurling gauntlets all over the place. I hasten to add that this was not always the case. There were short graceful speeches, often of a ceremonial type, done gently and elegantly, also written out. But I mostly remember the Meiklejohn fighting speech, and it was far removed from the conversational Meiklejohn. He was well received, enjoyed, admired in his oratorical role, but it was the side of him I liked least. I was uneasy, I think, at the change in the familiar voice, the almost strident insistence of tone. Perhaps I was simply unfamiliar with the vanishing tradition of oratory. Still . . . . Once, after one of his longer speeches, I remarked that I thought that it had ended anticlimactically, that I had noticed this about several of his speeches—a considerable letdown toward the end. "Of course," he said, "of course. I have an obligation to return the listener to the condition in which I found him." A characteristically surprising remark evoking the image of Meiklejohn taking his passengers on a wild roller-coaster ride, tapering off at the end, smiling and straightening their ties as they file out, handing their destinies, like transfers, back into their own hands.

Remembering Alexander Meiklejohn! It is unlikely that there will be a seventy-fifth reunion of the Experimental College. Soon enough there will be no one left who will remember the lifting of the spirits at the sight of his spare figure briskly entering the room. I am filled with a regret that he would laugh at. Have I not heard of mortality? Are we to be concerned about the persistence of fame? The accidents upon which that rests? Meiklejohn was a great man and, I admit, I do not want him to join the anonymous ranks of forgotten great men. Every generation must have them—men who stand out among their contemporaries by virtue of character, integrity, intelligence, vitality, who leave a deep mark on those whose lives they have touched and then are known no more, who have not left a permanent monument behind to reinvoke their presence. They are the fresh incarnations of the great human archetypes, as Alexander Meiklejohn was a great incarnation of the type of which Socrates was also an instance—the teacher who seems never to be off duty.